CW00566475

Art and the Power of Goodness

Photography

Almost all the art works, except external ones indicated or in the narration as author's, belong to former President John Agyekum Kufuor. Many were acquired between 2000-2018 and are now private or family. His interest, when I first explained the concept of text reflections alongside visuals, went a long way to motivate me to write a book like this. Apart from everything else, it adds up to an important side of his tenure in public life. This is a chip of a curatorial idea when I started work on the John A Kufuor Museum and Presidential Library in Kumasi around 2010 as its inaugural curator.

Once the works were identified, Jacob Nii Marley, a young heritage and visual anthropologist with the A.G. Leventis Digital Centre for African Culture at the University of Ghana was commissioned. With a detailed photographic sense as part of his broad skill set (which include digitalisation and graphic design), we spent hours and days at the former President's house as Marley took these images one after the other.

The complexity or otherwise of each work determined the average time needed, using a lighting system and adjustments that would bring out the intended effects in composition and expression. It had to be done patiently and correctly by this artist who was also an associate in museum work at the Norwegian University of Science and Technology in Trondheim and an alumnus of the British Museum's International Training Programme.

Art and the Power of Goodness

A Collection of
John Agyekum Kufuor

Ivor AGYEMAN-DUAH

Foreword by Gordon Brown

DigiBooks

Published in 2021 by
Digibooks Ghana Ltd.
P. O. Box BT1, Tema, Ghana
Tel: +233-303-414-720 / +233-246-493-842
Email: admin@digibookspublishing.com
Website: http://www.digibookspublishing.com

ISBN 978-9988-9029-9-5

Text © Ivor Agyeman-Duah 2021

All rights reserved; no part of this publication may be reproduced, stored
in a retrieval system, transmitted in any form or by any means, electronic,
mechanical, photocopying, recording, or otherwise, without the prior written
permission of the publishers.

Design and typesetting by Kwabena Agyepong

Contents

Acknowledgements

The times, from early March 2020, were uncertain in humanity's affliction with the Coronavirus. Global re-fashion of words became stronger and terminologies of Lockdown, Self-Quarantine, were expressions of survival. The discipline this brought, added to the self-imposed writer's life and so, the text and manuscript got completed in few months.

In his travels as a President and after, Kufuor always had a team including security. Whilst I was part of many, the memories from others at the office including, Adu Acheampong were helpful with a couple of artworks - which came from where and when? Among my collection of artworks is a set of *The Illustrated London News: The Ashantee War Sketches* which I acquired through the generosity of the distinguished literary jurist and editorial director, Margaret Busby OBE, FRSL and her brother, George Busby. Few of these paintings are used in textual illustrations in this book.

I will in essence like to thank all including of course, Jacob Nii Martey the book's designer and typesetter, Kwabena Agyepong, my regular editor, Sarah Apronti and the editorial staff of Digibooks.

My appreciation as well to Julie Hudson who has worked as a curator for African Collections at the British Museum for over twenty-five years. For ten years of this time, she also managed the Museum's Africa Programme, building collaborative partnerships with museums in East and West Africa. Her earlier reading of this work was as inspiring as her association with Ghana since 2007, working with colleagues in museums, universities and the wider heritage sector.

Foreword

I got to know of John Agyekum Kufuor when he was President of Ghana and I was serving as Prime Minister of the United Kingdom. We worked together on progressive policies, including education and primary and maternal health care in Ghana and Africa, as well as the other UN Millennium Development Goals. John was one of very few non-member leaders who attended G-8 meetings.

When he was elected as the first global leader to receive the Chatham House Prize of the Royal Institute of International Affairs, many of his accomplishments that were highlighted revolve around some of the visual art in this collection: how to work to address water scarcity in the Sahel, farm and agriculture products and commodity pricing in West Africa and the beautiful kente of his Ashanti and Ghanaian heritage in the textile business.

I was glad he was able to join me in 2016 in the work of the Global Citizenship Commission of eminent artists, Nobel prize winners, historians, philosophers and politicians in Edinburgh as we sought to re-align the UN fundamental rights for contemporary progress. We have also worked on advocacy platforms as recently as in May 2020 with the G-20 strategic engagements on the Covid-19 pandemics.

As a leader and one of the progressives of his generation in Africa and the world, this collection is most reflective of a global history shaped by Africa: we see beautiful colours of the Maasai in Kenya, the paintings of inspiration of post-Apartheid presented to him by other eminent leaders such as Nelson Mandela and Thabo Mbeki, a pottery in memory of the abolitionist, William Wilberforce from the Archbishop of York or from the East and Southeast Asia, vases that defined classical Chinese creativity, Korean textile and Mongolia violin instrument across generations of artists.

This selected collection, and the companion essays from his long-time biographer Ivor Agyeman-Duah, is itself a visual account of taste and history. And it comes at a time when Africa's contributions (and the larger Commonwealth of Nations in which Africa is such a prominent leader) to the creative industries is growing rapidly.

Rt Hon. Gordon BROWN,
UN Special Envoy for Global Education &
Former Prime Minster of the United Kingdom,
Fife, Scotland.
July, 2020.

Introduction

Art has always been part of Africa's power exhibitions. It is evidently on display in many palace architectures and interior decorations among major ethnic groups. Traditional leadership institutions prevailed for centuries before colonial rule and formal systems of record-keeping came. Before these, alphabets, proverbs and other folkloric media were in existence and are still. Whether it is metallurgy of art or portraits of kings and queens of centuries gone by, relics of their household items that have become part of palace antiquity, it had always been there, first as history before anything else. These also include patterns of cloth and their name-expressions. Art and history are mixed—of stools and chairs for palace, household elders, family heads and individuals carved differently.

These could be classified as institutional or leadership art. They were however not originally meant to be seen as art but utility elements for functional household or society's usages. It had only been with time, when their utility values had become less so because of either new inventions or advanced forms of prototype, that they tended to have or assumed artistic dimensions.

Resistance and Cooperation

1874- Ashanti. The last Anglo-Ashanti War was led on the Ashanti side by Yaa Asantewaa, queen mother of Ejisu in 1900. In colonial historiography, the role of communication is subsumed. The talking drums of the Akans or the Xylophone of the Dagaaba and the Sisaala in northern Ghana, were for strategic military communication which could not be de-codified easily by the British. In tracking down anti-colonialists like Yaa Asantewaa in the deep forest, they installed telegraph wires on one of the grounds of the fiercest battles along the Prah road in Ashanti. It helped in her arrest.

The Illustrated London News war artist in Kumasi in 1874, did this pencil painting of two British technicians being aided in fixing the poles; we see telegraph wires on the ground of this forested neighbourhood of five houses and possibly more. Other people carry on their chores on the left.

They could be similar in many cultures within Africa and also Europe. The *atɛnnɛ* of the Asantes of Ghana is leader of providers of the king's lighting system at the palace. They always ensured, in the olden days that, light or wood energy was provided against darkness with a lantern, and especially when the king was about or in procession. There was a similar establishment in Pre-Victorian British Houses of Parliament and other European traditional institutions. Like the *atɛnnɛ* at the Adae festival or Big Akwasidae Festival, they were on full display at the opening of Parliament or other ceremonial occasions.

Public art—of recognition through statues in public or social spaces evolved from histories of most societies. The carving of Yoruba gods in palaces could be full of the attributes of their goodness prayed to for procreation and increase of the matri-clan, fertility of soil for plentiful harvest and others. Among the Ibos of Nigeria, the wearing of masks, which came in different shapes and expressions had serious religious connotation in for instance Chinua Achebe's, *Arrow of God*. In clay figurines in parts of West Africa including Ivory Coast, the burial of kings in the ancient times was preceded by the making of a portrait of the corpses as close in resemblance as possible. The portraits would be exposed to the sun to dry and later roasted in a traditional oven to ensure eternal preservation.

Thus, depending on the environmental conditions in the tropics, wintry conditions of Europe or what is called the West, artists have found materials to preserve memories. The tropics with abundant timber led to wooden sculpture in West and Central Africa as much as the Cedars of Lebanon made great interior decoration in the temple that Solomon built in Jerusalem.

These evolved or got enhanced through exposure to other cultures, civilisations and interests in their items for art. Paintings in Europe—whether from the old masters of Italy, Britain, Spain or The Netherlands graduated into photography when the latter was invented. It might have reduced dependence on painting with its longevity of creation but it did not kill it. It continually enjoyed huge patronage alongside the new invention because of fashion and the prestige and conservative aroma of the past. Photography may be cheaper today, even professional ones, not to talk of the easy technology of the smartphone. Yet, it is easy to imagine that when photography emerged, many at the time thought that was the end of painting as an art form.

Art collection by individuals or institutions has been as old as art creation. The British Museum was established in 1753 but far away from it, by 1809 in Ashanti, of whom the British would engage in five wars for colonisation, the West African kingdom's King Osei Bonsu knew the value of art. He was cosmopolitan in ideas and had built a huge museum called The Aban. British and American journalists who visited Kumasi the capital found it amazing. They were from

London's, *Daily Telegraph, The London Times,* and from the United States' *The New York Herald* whose correspondent wrote: "yataghans and scimitars of Arabic make, Damask bed-curtains and counterpanes. English engravings, an oil painting of a gentleman, an old uniform of a West Indian soldier, brass blunderbuss, prints from illustrated newspapers…" [1]

Some Eurocentric commentary argued that Osei Bonsu possibly had heard of the British Museum and wanted to have a similar one. It implies that he was not capable of understanding art and its aesthetics, let alone preservation. Yet, we are also talking of a kingdom that from the early 1700s, came into being as an imperial power interested apart from power consolidation, in the best cultural practices of the vanquished.

The Aban gave an idea of trade relations between Ashanti and its neighbours and of international trade relations. It is known that at the peak of the empire, they had traded with merchants from North Africa and the Middle East and Asia either through primary transactions or third party.

The German art historian, Martha J Ehrlich who has written extensively of stolen art from Ashanti, around this particular period recounted a well-known story of how the British, Sir Garnet Wolseley who got to Kumasi in 1873-74 together with others, West Indians and other Africans under his command, ransacked the palace of its art and other treasures:

"The prize agents worked one whole night and complained of being assigned an impossible task in the amount of time given them because there were many rooms in the palace that were almost filled with things…." Henry Brackenbury, who accompanied the prize agents, wrote that, "thousands of things were left behind that would be worth fabulous sums in cabinet at home." [2]

Many of these items, some of which are at the British Museum and scattered in parts of Europe and in private collection, go back into the 1700s and are among items preserved by cultural nationalists engaged in the campaign for their reparation.

Many of these palace regalia remained and were recreated even if, as I say, their functional values today are not as significant as before. Kings and chiefs, palace attendants and officials since the 1800s, have been protective of many of these systems and items as part and parcel of their cultural inheritance and civilisations including family treasures - of gold, diamond and precious items from generations. Wealth had previously been calculated on the quantum of such inheritance and during puberty rites and marriage ceremonies, young women had been dressed in or had worn some of these, whether as earrings, bracelets or gold sandals.

⬠ Military Camp

1874 - Ashanti. This is a pristine art of a British military camp at the Prah. Obviously on a main road or pathway, it shows the camp architecture (wooden built with raffia materials and palm as cover) of which sits the commander or captain. The scenery of two tents, with armed soldiers in front and behind the wooden barricade, looks like an occupation with a family comfortably passing by from a farm with home needs.

Art among the Akans of Ghana as it is in many other places, could be created from their philosophical beliefs. Language Art is of a symbol which could generate thousands of words or a book. An *Adinkra* symbol such as *Gye Nyame*, which means "Except God" could be painted and also spoken of. It is therefore dual, visual and spoken art and of the essence of life and challenges, the poverty of the individual and nation, limitation of wisdom and scientific inquiry are all possible through God.

An African proverb (of the Wolof ethnic group within Senegal, Gambia and Mauritania): *If you know the beginning well the end will not trouble you,* is the historical past, analysis in economic history, political transitions and family history by which sometimes wealth is claimed or lost. [3] It is very easy to get an African artist to paint or draw to this philosophical effect. It is similar to another that Chinua Achebe popularised even as he was not sure whether it is a Maasai proverb or from which African society - *Until the lions learn to tell their story, the history of hunting would always glorify the hunter.* A favourite of post-colonial rhetoric of politicians and literary ideologues, Africans should, it implies, learn to tell their own stories, interpret their own histories otherwise, outsiders and especially European histories could easily justify colonial rule.

The art of gold-weights was not original art and among the Ashanti connected to its monetary system. They are many and as varied as the Egyptian hieroglyphics; their interpretation could be as different. Art could have and has always had a universal appeal and does border-crossing. Though Picasso never visited the Congo, he spoke of its great creativity and art form.

One of the most interesting art interpretations I have encountered —and I have written about it in *Shepherds of New Dawn* (2020)— is the African-American novelist and playwright, James Baldwin's. In the artwork, 'Yoruba Man with a Bicycle' he wrote:

> This is something. This has got to be contemporary. He's really going to town. It's very jaunty, very authoritative. His errand might prove to be impossible. He is challenging something- or something has challenged him…he's apparently a very proud and silent man. He's dressed sort of polyglot. Nothing looks like it fits him too well. [4]

As I reviewed Baldwin's own review, my interpretation of his interpretation was that, "Baldwin never knew the artist but his work and therefore never knew whether the artist wanted to create a challenged individual or what was on his mind. His interpretation could be fictitious to some extent but that fictional interpretation was also born out of the fact that indeed, this Yoruba sculpture artist is a subject of "all art is local."[5]

Art interpretation could be beyond the local. The international market or buyers could also make sense of what they purchase or interpret.

Benin Bronze

2014 - Benin, Nigeria. From the mid 1800s, British colonial policy was aimed at icono-clastism and philistinism towards colonial rebellion. The period between 1870 and the 1890s saw the destruction of many cultural and precious royal regalia in Ashanti and the Edo people of Benin in Nigeria. When the Benin bronze portraits first got to Britain and other parts of Europe, the wealth of Africa's creativity received major attention.

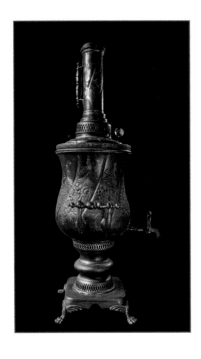

Lamp

West Africa. Long before lamps like this, there were the lanterns which centuries ago were popular in Europe and later on Africa as read and depicted in novels such as Margaret Atwood's *The Handmaid's Tale* or Chinua Achebe's *Things Fall Apart*. They generated the needed light for domestic usage. Energy had also been through forest wood and coal.

Interpretation, of which I will engage in a lot in the latter part of this work or even speculation which has a higher level of uncertainty, could be different from authentication. These could be the terrain of specialists and art detectives but the uninitiated could also venture.

◦◦⊱——··•◦•   ‖   •◦··——⊰◦◦

By March 2020, Sotheby's London which was established in 1774, had grown as an international art auction house in Paris, New York and in Asia, Hong Kong and India, with eighty offices in forty countries. It had its Global Fine Art Division, not to talk of online interior market design.

In a press release that month on *Modern and Contemporary African Art Return to Sotheby's London*, there was an interesting bit about the work of the distinguished Nigerian artist, Ben Enwonwu, sometimes described as "Africa's most influential artist of the C20th" who passed on in 1994. It read:

> The sale will be led by a radiant early painting by Nigerian master Ben Enwonwu. Until recently, the enigmatic sitter had been known only as the 'Nigerian princess' but, upon close examination, Sotheby's specialists noticed intricate details which led them to believe the sitter could be Princess Judith Safinet 'Sefi' Atta. The sitter's blouse is fashioned from the Okene cloth produced by the Ebira women of Sefi's

hometown. Upon contacting Sefi's daughter, the artist Obi Okigbo, she revealed that her mother knew Enwonwu well: *"When Hannah sent me the photo of the painting, I felt like I was like looking at a portrait of myself. The family resemblance is remarkable.* [6]

The release goes on, and this is where the specialist, very sure of his craft, comes in again. Speaking about the work, Hannah O'Leary, said:

> *Stories like this are the reason I love what I do. Not only have we come across an outstanding early painting by Ben Enwonwu, we have also uncovered a moving story about Sefi herself - an accomplished force in the fight for women's right to education in Nigeria and beyond. This portrait sits right at the crux of the cultural and artistic landscape of 20th century Nigeria. As the battle for a unified identity intensified, so did the passions of the writers, poets and painters who were working side by side – Ben Enwonwu, Chinua Achebe, John Pepper Clarke, and the poet Christopher Okigbo, the latter of whom Sefi married. It has been an honour to hear this story, and I am grateful to Sefi's daughter Obi for letting me in.* [7]

Obi Okigbo's father was the poet, Christopher Okigbo who died in the course of the Biafra War in Nigeria and whose mother is the prominent educationist, diplomat and subject of the painting. She is also the auntie of the award-winning novelist of among others, *Everything Good Will Come*, Sefi Atta. The family's artistic horizon is far and wide. Notwithstanding the firmness of the specialist (even as 'could be' is used all the same) in the matter of authentication, some close family members do not seem to be so sure. And at the time, they would not want the subject at her age to be engaged in an exercise of validation. What makes the judgement of an art detective or specialist overcome close family members?

Like all goods and commodities of monetary value, the art market could also do with speculation which, together with interpretation and authentication, make it more of a world. But it is also true that time as it rolls away, could lead to a momentary lapse of memory or forgetfulness of small details which count. If the subject does not wholly remember, and family members were not born at the time or if even so, there will be an avenue for the specialist.

There is a good extent to which art relates to politics and power. The dressings of power are through art from thrones of kings and queens, and from Buckingham Palace through to colonial ones of old. Many modern politicians have taken inspiration from histories, artistic expressions and the spiritual inclinations they give. The role of some immediate post-colonial artists was in the creation of new sovereign architectures - national flags, coat of arms, presidential stools, symbols of parliamentary and judiciary authority.

◆ Modern Canvas

December 2018 – Accra, Ghana. A unique artwork using four different materials for the canvas: a black metal backbone support with ceramic edges, a frontal ceramic plain with two glass surfaces at both ends. In the middle is ceramic mix with wood and three strings of light ring metal and intricate calligraphy. The use of waste products including plastics and other metals for canvas in contemporary Ghanaian art is most exemplified in the works of the artist, Ibrahim Mahama. This is however the work of Ken Wurah, who also uses text to explain his motivation.

Royals who from the 1930s had formal European education still retained respect for traditional institutions. Some, like Jomo Kenyatta the first independent president of Kenya, had scholarships to study in England through traditional institutions in Kenya. In the Gold Coast to become Ghana from 1957, nationalists, lawyers and cultural activists and historians – Mensah Sarbah, Casely Hayford, J.B. Danquah and later Alex Atta Yaw Kyerematen, J.H. Kwabena Nketia and Oku Ampofo were from royal households or connected through other ways. On their return with anthropological and literary skills, they delineated many artistic creations adding value to them. Some, unlike Baldwin, knew of the artists in their small communities and so they could get into their minds.

The most visible scholarship for modern education in Kumasi however was the Asanteman Council Scholarship instituted by the King of Asante, Agyeman Prempeh II through which many notables got trained as lawyers, engineers, doctors, university administrators. Some became ministers of state and prominent politicians.

Others (not in this scholarship category) who emerged most famous of all would include, Kofi Diawuo, son of the Oyokohene of Kumasi, the ruling clan of Ashanti and the Akan. Born from a wealthy cocoa and soft commodities middle class family from the matrilineal home of Apagyafie (of Nana Ama Dapaah, mother) and the father, Oyokohene Nana Kwadwo Agyekum, his sister, Agnes Addo Kufuor would later marry the King - Agyeman Prempeh II. Kofi Diawuo would become the President of the Republic of Ghana - as John Agyekum Kufuor. His exposure to Ashanti cultural nuances was all around him including court and judiciary structure that would influence his two terms, eight-year successful rule of the country.

I had known him as an art enthusiast who appreciates music composition, visual expression and photography, endlessly talking about the ones he likes. Some of the collections were gifts or what he brought home from visits to traditional architectural buildings in Ethiopia, north of Lebanon or encounters with Islamic history at Middle Eastern museums. He virtually designed his palatial retirement home in Aburi near Accra in the Eastern region, including interior choice items of Akan art and Middle Eastern and oriental mix. He once ran a ceramic and architecture related - brick manufacturing business. If he can be called a collector in an artistic sense, it is with watches: Rolex, Longlines, Cartier, Timeless, Hublot, etc, etc and their intricate and imposing designs.

In 2007, I did a major 400-paged biography on him, *Between Faith and History* which was internationally well-received. Two editions - one by the Africa World Press in Trenton, New Jersey and the other by Ayebia Clarke Publishing Company in Oxfordshire, have since seen many reprints. As he was also a president, the book focused on his presidential ambitions, tenure and public policy. I have also been asked by many why I had not done another or an extension to cover his post-presidency. That period brought him many honours as he established The John A Kufuor Foundation of which I served as initial curator.

The impact of *Between Faith and History* overshadows another work, *Africa - A Miner's Canary into the C21st - Essays on Economic Governance* published by Bookcraft in Ibadan, Nigeria. Though a collection of personal essays, parts of that book look at that post-presidency but still in the realm of politics and economics. Politics and international affairs have always been his pre-occupation since he served as a deputy minister in the Government of Ghana's Second Republic under Dr. K.A. Busia in the late 1960s.

Kufuor's artistic inclination has been a consciousness on my part though it had no appropriate space under the circumstance of my association before this work. It was however, during a visit to his home in early 2020 that two things struck me. The first was a pair of Benin bronze-works of a man and a woman. The complicated metal artwork - of facial stratification of famous personage, arrested the attention of many wherever they found them and in whatever size. It does not matter how shoddy some of the replicas are from the original smelting. The other art work was a digital painting of Exeter College, one of the constituent colleges of the University of Oxford where

Kufuor studied Politics, Philosophy and Economics and which sits on a broad glass-base among others.

My original idea was to do a data entry of these before he and other family members forgot their origins - who brought what as gift, the occasions and where he himself bought some. As ideas sometimes die, this perished and got replaced by another - the concept of this book.

◁▤──‥•◦▯ IV ▯◦•‥──▤▷

This book is a selection of over seventy works from his Accra airport residential home. At 82, he sits in a huge single weather sofa with feet usually stretched on an artistic foot-rest from the northern part of Ghana. In the afternoons he receives visitors and international diplomats, some of whom are addicted to seeing the photography of power-play with the eminence of the contemporary world - the Pontiff of Rome, Kofi Annan, Gordon Brown, Tony Blair and philosophers such as Amartya Sen and Kwame Anthony Appiah.

An unintended gallery in a double-chamber space of a former president of his stature may not be extraordinary. However, these are not just photo-ops but people he had intimately worked with around the world. On his eightieth birthday and because I had been part of his office, I wrote an essay reflecting on some of this photography:

> In October 2018, the Exeter College of the University of Oxford had a fascinating exhibition on the writings and archives of its alumnus novelist, J.R. R. Tolkien whose 1949 famous novel, *The Lord of the Rings* is considered great literature. Its filmography adaptation series, broke the box office in excess of $870 million winning multiple Academy Awards. It is reminiscent in contemporary terms of J.K. Rowling's the Harry Potter fantasy series.
>
> In the next couple of weeks, the College will also unveil a full photographic portrait of another alumnus it deems distinguished enough - former President John Agyekum Kufuor at its Learning Commons at Cohen Quad, a recently renovated centuries old building. Kufuor will join the philosopher and Kwame Nkrumah's literary friend, William Abraham the first African and to date, the only one to be elected a Fellow of All Souls College of Oxford in 1959, to be so honoured.
>
> Kufuor's honour comes ten years after his presidency and is propitious in the sense that history is always framed in time and often coincidental. A sort of a foreign affairs president like Jawaharlal Nehru in India before him, Kufuor's post- presidency from 2009-2018, first saw him assume the chairmanship of the Alliance for Africa Foundation which was partly set up by the Milan City Council for education infrastructure development in Africa.

He subsequently became Ambassador of the World Food Programme in Rome and chairman of the Interpeace in Geneva which operates in seventeen post-war countries. He also joined a Commission to look into re-empowering the World Bank for the 21st century, which was chaired by the former President of Mexico and Director of the Yale Center for the Study of Globalization, Ernesto Zedillo. It included the then Director-General of the WTO- Pascal Lamy and the President of JICA then, Sadko Ogata.

From 2010, he would be involved with ten other international organisations of exotic company such as the Global Citizenship Commission chaired by former UK Prime Minister, Gordon Brown. Members of the commission included former US Treasury Secretary, Robert Rubin, the historian Emma Rothschild, Nobel laureate Mohamed El Baradei and the Archbishop of Canterbury, Rowan Williams. They were to review the UN Universal Declaration of Human Rights for a 21st Century World. He would also be involved in an eminent preparatory committee meeting to help influence the agenda of the G20 Seoul Summit in 2010.

Kufuor's international engagements apart from multilateral ones, were as envoy of the UN Secretary-General, leader of the Commonwealth and African Union electoral observer missions and co-director with President Jimmy Carter on electoral contest and associated conflicts. Speaking engagements, whether from the London Speaker Bureau or elsewhere, could run continuously for a month: addressing packed auditoriums at the Weill Cornell Medical College in

⬟ Kufuor as Police Commander

London, UK. Walking around Central London one day, Kufuor, in the company of a security detail came across a London Metropolitan Police Officer who on recognising him as President of Ghana, saluted and gave him his duty cap in respect. Being an officer, this symbolism to a Commander-in-Chief of a sovereign defense force was well-received. On his return to Ghana, an art company - Senel Design and Construction which deals in art products and uses waste plastic and glass, had incidentally done a bust of him in suit. The cap fitted easily.

New York on some of his successful social and economic policies like the National Health Insurance Scheme; as inaugural lecturer of The Legatum Center at the Massachusetts Institute of Technology (MIT) in Cambridge; as commemorative guest speaker at universities in Seoul and influencing public policy from Japan to land reforms in Dar es Salaam; as counsel to Maasai leaders and cultural conservationists in rural Kenya and sharing thoughts with decision makers of the African Development Bank in a series of guest lectureship in Tunisia on political economy.

In between the many engagements were the awards and appreciations, whether a doctorate degree from the ancient University of Edinburgh or as World Food Prize laureate speaking at the UK Houses of Parliament on food security in Africa on behalf of the Partnership for Child Development of the Imperial College London; or reward for his mediating role in the Kenya crisis of 2007, La Côte d' Ivoire and Liberia.

In 2011, President Alassane Quattara invited Kufuor as Guest of Honour through the Interpeace and publicly said whilst inaugurating the country's Truth and Reconciliation Commission that, "Today marks all your (Kufuor) efforts in seeking to bring peace to La Côte d'Ivoire and we cannot thank you enough."

The international leadership portfolios also included being the first chair of the high-level Geneva-based Sanitation and Water for All which looks at sanitation and water as critical factors of economic growth in the developing world beyond Africa and into parts of Asia and the Caribbean.

These were all reflective of the successful public policy and foreign engagements during his presidency and as chairman of the African Union.

Whilst these were obviously gratifying for his global stewardship, the home-front in Ghana was a stormy transition between 2009-2010. His party had unexpectedly lost power to the NDC, led by Prof. John Atta Mills. Tension and even recrimination became part of the swan song. The Chinery Hesse Committee which he had put together to look into future presidential emoluments had become controversial of what entitlements should be given former presidents. Prof. Mills set up a new commission to review that report downwards and attendant media reportage was overbearingly negative against the earlier one.

Kufuor's anticipated retirement office at the Ridge government enclave was the target of a mob attack should he use it. A youth organisation was claiming it as indigenous to the people of the area. That incident shocked many participants at an African Presidential Archives and Research Centre conference which Kufuor was chairing at the time in Tanzania. Eventually, in the course of what seemed a regular effrontery, his office was relocated to his home at Airport West in Accra.

Certainly, the times were against him at home. For what was considered by analysts as even within reach - the Mo Ibrahim Prize alluded him in a mirage fashion. I remember a call from a BBC correspondent who intimated that their investigation indicated the Prize would be given to Kufuor in an announcement to be made by its chair, the late Kofi Annan the following day. The BBC was therefore sending to Accra a correspondent from Abidjan who would interview Kufuor afterwards.

Very early the following morning, the correspondent called to say that the Committee had decided not to award the prize that year to any of the highly eligible candidates, among them, President Thabo Mbeki of South Africa. The announcement to be made that afternoon, he said, would confirm this. It did confirm that to the joy of the new powers in Accra as there was also relief among some within Kufuor's own party with not a residual disliking of him over the ages.

You do not win all the time in politics but time defines who you become in the context of its ticking. From the global engagements of 2009 and the concurrent stormy times at home, there now seems to be a settlement. It is always the case whichever way one looks at it. The personality debasement by neophytes of the newly baptised into politics, their youthful philistine attitude to decorum is even ensured by time in history.

The "Ifs' of history itself are always a primordial element of little relevance at the end but difficult to refrain from its sometimes speculative powers of the past, and of the present. 'If' Vladimir Lenin had not travelled by train in 1917 from Zurich to Petrograd in Russia or had been killed on arrival from this exile journey by train, would the Bolshevik Revolution have changed the world? And would Nkrumah who counted that as one of the

● Great Commission

2016 - Scotland, United Kingdom. Members of the Global Citizenship Commission include leaders who helped resolve some human development challenges of the early C21st It was "under the leadership of British Prime Minister, Gordon Brown and the auspices of NYU's Global Institute for Advanced Study, to re-examine the spirit and stirring words of The Universal Declaration of Human Rights." They are leaders in economics, economic history and finance, peace-building, theology and religion, politics, philosophy and others : K. Anthony Appiah, Laurel Bellows, Nicolas Berggruen, Paul Boghossian, Gordon Brown (Chair), Craig Calhoun, Wang Chenguang, Mohamed ElBaradei, Fonna Forman, Andrew Forrest, Ronald M. George, Asma Jahangir, John Kufuor, Graça Machel, Catherine O'Regan, Ricken Patel, Emma Rothschild, Robert Rubin, Jonathan Sacks, Kailash Satyarthi, Klaus Schwab, Amartya Sen, John Sexton, Robert Shrum, Jeremy Waldron, Joseph Weiler, Rowan Williams, Diane C. Yu (Executive Director).

greatest events of the time have been inspired? Would March 6 1957 or another date be our independence day? And would Kufuor have been in line over forty years after?

Kufuor has a mental rotation on political leadership, models and their evolution. In that sense, his occupation is not gone at a good age of eighty but within historical reckoning in its measure for measure.

Time! Memory!! History!!! [8]

Few of these art works are external, that is from the author, and are there only to help in certain narratives. Otherwise they – from over twenty countries and forty societies within them - reflect global art - West Africa and the Sahel- Nigeria, Ivory Coast, Burkina Faso, Mali, Cameroon and also South Africa; from north of Africa into the Maghreb- Morocco, the eternal city of Rome and into Jerusalem and the Middle East. There are Asian oriental vases of varying sizes from South Korea and China. Each of the ten essays has art works to complement and support the narration of biographical details, perspective on contemporary art and even observation and concerns of artists and how increasingly, the cultural or creative economy is driving into the mainstream in Africa.

Ivor Agyeman-Duah,
Accra,
April, 2020.

Chapter One

A Sorcerer's Apprentice:
Lesson in Portrait Painting

The Governing Board of the Exeter College of the University of Oxford decided in 2018 to honour former President John Agyekum Kufuor with his photographic portrait decoration at the College. One of the oldest at the University, it had celebrated its 800th anniversary under its Rector, Frances Cairncross the economist and former Managing Editor of, *The Economist* magazine. The decision carried on under her successor, Sir Richard Trainor who had headed King's College London in a previous occupation and is also a well-known historian and university administrator. He had, prior to this, as I indicated in the Introduction, supervised a huge exhibition on the writings and papers of J.R.R. Tolkien, the famous author of *The Lord of the Rings* as well as the best-selling novelist, Sir Philip Pullman of *The Good Man Jesus and the Scoundrel Christ.*

Kufuor was not the first Ghanaian or African to study at the College. The international diplomat, Alex Quaison-Sackey who became the first black man to serve as the President of the United Nations General Assembly from 1964-65 and also as Ghana's High Commissioner to The Court of St. James's in London was there. Two Exeter College alumni who were famous British Africanists and anthropologists who were also there were, R.S. Rattray and E.E. Evans-Pritchard.

Rattray had studied under the Rector of the College, R.R. Marett from 1909 and it is said that it was Marett who after the famous Scot Governor of the Gold Coast, Sir Gordon Guggisberg had dinner with him recommended Rattray (already working in the Gold Coast colonial administration) as government anthropologist in Ashanti part. He had written and published between 1914-1916, *Ashanti Proverbs*. His posting would be fundamental to their major nineteenth century history. Rattray was also known in Southern Africa.

E.E. Evans-Pritchard would also work in West Africa including the Gold Coast. Again it would be another anthropologist and

Accomplishment

2020 - Oxford, London, Britain. This portrait by the Greek figurative painter Aris Raissis, is named *Accomplishment* by the author. It took four months into the second quarter of 2020 to get it done. It evolved from a black and white photographic image commissioned by the Exeter College of the University of Oxford. It was and still is, to honour its alumnus and an African president. Its hanging abode would be Cohen Quad and was originally to celebrate Kufuor's eightieth birthday. The evolution into this painting as we read in the first chapter, was inspired by the Great Dutch Masters in the 17th century. It is the first painting of an African leader at a place of honour in Exeter College's 800-year old history.

historian alumnus of the College, Malcolm McLeod who also knew Evans-Pritchard from Exeter College in the mid 1960s who would help to set-up the Manhyia Palace Museum in Kumasi decades after. Author of *The Ashanti,* he would in 2019 deliver the RP Baffour Memorial Lectures at the Kwame Nkrumah University of Science and Technology partly on his work and times in Ghana. [9]

Kufuor's exceptional recognition partly has to do with the fact of the College not being Balliol, a production machine of prime ministers and foreign presidents at Oxford but as the College says, of his rewarding stewardship in Ghanaian and global politics.

❖⊰————••❖❙   ❙❙   ❙❖••————⊱❖

The black and white photo for the honours was taken on a visit to Oxford and at a conservative space in front of a wooden door with black metal strips as part of the design. With a choice of background of old wooden doors, it shone light on the facial features of the subject. But that was photography and the intent of the photographer. We wanted a painted version of this official choice and that was a different process altogether. Painting takes time and is elaborate including pre-conditions of size of canvass, colour mix and the more delicate balance of not being painted from a single image.

The London based painter born in Cairo but of Greek origin, Aris Raissis was settled on to do that. The 58-year old, whose family had been part of the establishment in Egyptian politics, had himself through art, indulged in royalty with such works as the commissioned portrait of HRH Crown Prince Alexander of Yugoslavia which was unveiled in the presence of Queen Elizabeth II at London's Claridge's. His works had also been exhibited and sold in Europe and the Middle East apart from having been used for tutorial engagements with budding artists from royal background in Saudi Arabia or the Indian middle class.

At his Wimbledon home close to the village, I had enjoyed other paintings in digital formats when he was artist-in-residence at Leighton House Museum, Kensington where he did a series of paintings for Opera Holland Park. With works in homes and public spaces in Egypt, Italy, France, Mexico, Greece, Germany, Kuwait, Azerbaijan, Norway and the United States, his confidence is about him and his school of art philosophy with it. His career intention from the beginning was "to concentrate on figurative painting, portraiture and still life." And that, he believes, is best achieved when one attempts "to reinstate the techniques of the Old Masters, whilst at the same time, selecting contemporary subject matter."

Kufuor first met him at the unveiling of the portrait of William Abraham at the All Souls College of the Faithful at Oxford. Raissis'

Original:

This was the original beautiful black and white photograph.
The work of a painter as it is, is different from a photographer's
with resolution of details: colour choice and mix. This includes
the tie colouration and free space to focus on the subject. An
obstruction of space in painting, could in photography be an
aesthetic delight.

A Resolution:

Raissis in further facial resolution with a projection
from the original black and
white portrait.

portrait of Abraham in 2018 marked a significance of African scholarship presence at the University. The first black Rhodes Scholar in 1959 had inspired many African scholars of the 1960s since he won the prize at 25.

When Kufuor's black and white photographic portrait was reviewed by Raissis, his premise was that, "composition is so important especially when portraying on a solitary, standing figure." This he has known since he studied at The Chelsea School of Fine Art and The Byam Shaw School of Fine Art. The school people studied at sometimes matter to them and he is proud of his training. He has his own level of respect for such established ones like the Slade School of Fine Art at the University College of London (UCL), as he believes others are catching up.

Over lunch in Wimbledon, he emphasised and would follow up with a mail which explains that, "the black and white photograph you emailed me certainly brings out an elegance of President Kufuor, but at the same time he is lost due to the amount of space around him."

Does space or spot of a photographer's choice matter so much? It does to him as a painter because the subject is not the surrounding. "The door behind him resembles the type that could have been used in a fortress or for a prison. In my opinion, this would look somewhat aggressive if included in the painting. The plants are a distraction."

The composition, he suggested, should "remain simple and to the point. A plain background that consists of a series of tones from dark to light would help enhance President Kufuor's presence."

And painting and outcome is not just the abstract art of it but the personality defines that particular outcome. Since Kufuor is tall in stature, "I can" he explained with a voice completely devoid of any Greco-Egyptian tonal betrayal, "afford to create a chiaroscuro effect on his body. This means that the highest area would be his head and the top section of his torso." Chiaroscuro in technicality is light and shade on the subject of painting and was in this particular instance, to create a dramatic effect. For "as the viewer's eye travels downwards, a shadow would set in, so as to, introduce a certain amount of drama."

That was a device Raissis told me was used especially by the Great Dutch Masters in the 17th century to "help the viewer to concentrate on the head. Rembrandt was certainly an artist who used this method in portrait painting."

You can see in the evolution - from a reverse side of how the black and white photo had come about. To make it worthy, the tie colour had to change using other photos of Kufuor in yellow tie as inspiration. You would also realise that the third photo that Raissis resolved from the original shows a clearer and nearer facial expression. It is better than the distant portrait for the purpose of painting.

idea

illuminated

in shadow

Having a concentrated shadow at the bottom of the painting allows the legs to appear soft and not just look like stilts.

The most intense section is the area around the head.

Even though the figure is standing at rest, the painting will contain the feeling of movement due to the introduction of shadows.

⬠ A Sketch:

This is a mental pen sketch Raissis developed in contemplation of the final expression on canvass.

What comes to mind is, does the racial background of an artist like Raissis in his painting of Kufuor or the Nigerian Ben Enwonwu in that of Queen Elizabeth II influence an outcome? Enwonwu had been given the MBE in 1955 for his contribution to the arts in Nigeria by the British colonial establishment. The following year, he became the first African artist to receive a royal commission to do a bronze statue of the Queen. In a photograph of Enwonwu and the Queen viewing together the statue, she is said to have liked it so much that she bought other works by Ben.

Did the art commentators who made references to having made the Queen look a little black have a point or nothing more than an academic debate? Enwonwu had been trained in European art movements including symbolism and techniques. It was however, his earlier training in traditional Igbo aesthetics by family that made him an artist first. [10]

By 1989, Enwonwu had come to the conclusion that an artist does not need to box himself into a school of thought or limit his imagination. It implies that if Raissis can make techniques of The Dutch Masters work better for him in a portrait of Kufuor, he should have no inhibitions. There should be no Pan Africanism, Eurocentrism or Americanism when Enwonwu said these by implication:

> I will not accept an inferior position in the art world nor
> have my art called African because I have not correctly and

properly given expression to my reality. I have consistently fought against this kind of philosophy because it is bogus.

European artists like Picasso, Braque and Vlaminck were influenced by African art. Everybody sees that and is not opposed to it. But when they see African artists who are influenced by European art and technique, they expect that the African would stick to his tradition even if he bends down to copy them. I do not copy traditional art. I like what I see in the works like Giacometti but I do not copy them. But I would not be influenced by Giacometti, because he was influenced by my ancestors. [11]

Over three decades since Ben argued this way, the Slade School of Fine Art at the UCL are encouraging students to bring on board their own creative ethos with little inhibitions of how to practise their profession. At the end, they say that beauty lies in the eyes of the beholder. And the market sometimes becomes invariably the final arbiter.

Chapter Two

A Woman's Tender Care

Kufuor met and later married then Theresa Mensah whilst they were both studying in the United Kingdom. He was combining law on the one hand, and politics, economics and philosophy at Oxford on the other. She was doing nursing in Edinburgh at whose famous Edinburgh University their elder grandson – one of thirteen, is now studying Engineering. She is also known as the sister of the undoubtedly eminent Ghanaian economist of his time, J.H. Mensah. With brothers and a husband mostly in the eyes of public service and storm she, a musical artist and a Catholic chorister, has always

⬠ Theresa

1950s. Ghana. The beauty and innocence of girlhood. Theresa was one of the few from her generation to have been trained abroad in the late 1950s. Though Africa's cultural expectations of women education were low, some went against the grain.

The Ashanti says: *Obaa da obarima akyi* - A woman lies behind a man or in more nuanced form, a man always takes first place, but it is the woman who backs him up. [41]

Another one says that she who combines beauty with other attributes makes her life and marriage successful, otherwise it is less so.

Obaa de feefe nko ara ko awaree a, onnya - If a woman uses 'beauty' only to get married, she will not be successful. In plain language, you need more than good looks to succeed in life. [42]

A Modernist

Ghana. A beautiful woman displays her body contours in new fashion as she sits on a *Gye Nyame* symbolised stool. It is made of bronze from Ghana. A conservative African man who believes that a woman should more than cover her beauty, could interpret this leisure image unkindly in proverbial terms.

Obaa kwadwofoo na otena afikyire pene kotekom - A lazy woman who sits in the backyard asks for sex or if you are not busy, you leave yourself time to reflect on unsatisfied desires. [43]

been a private individual; a trait found among their five children. It somehow reinforces an Akan customary belief: children may resemble their father but their real family is the mother's.

Now octogenarian, Mrs. Kufuor's taste is still musical. On the two occasions that I had seen her hilariously over her usual, it had been music that had done that. One was in Milan in Italy in 2010. Kufuor had completed his two terms as president and had been invited to chair the Alliance for Africa Foundation. It was his first travel after leaving office. The organisers got VIP tickets for Mr. and Mrs. Kufuor and son, John Addo Kufuor (Chief Kufuor) for the operatic concert at the over 300-year old La Scala opera house. The world renowned place has seen its artists and other singers perform and gain stamps of achievement. The performance of the La Scala Theatre Chorus led by its conductor, was like a huge robot in the evening. It overwhelmed her and other VIPs that included, as we later realised, President Wade of Senegal.

Of the launch of the Alliance for Africa Foundation itself, the organisers had invited the Malian maestro, Salifu Keita who as expected, almost brought the roof of the venue down. People were on their feet, having been induced by that hedonistic voice and geometric dancehall movements. He brought his full fame to bear. His salutation was to an African personality and wife who had served their time well and made Africa proud, he said.

It gave me a good impression of what Mrs. Kufuor was really interested in. The belly of politics had almost destroyed her infant family and this is clearest in a forthcoming work by Kufuor in his prison memoirs:

> My youngest son, Kofi Owusu Afriyie was born while I was in detention. I remember the day Theresa brought him to the prison to see me. In the visiting area, there was a tall shelf across the tables, separating prisoners from guests. She had to pass the baby over the shelf so I could hold him. She was trying to be strong for the children but in her eyes and voice I could feel her loneliness. Not only was she doing her best to visit me regularly, she was also attending to her brother JH Mensah. He was detained in another jail in Nsawam, a long journey to the north east of Accra. The children recounted to me the outings their mother had taken them on. Although Theresa struggled financially, earning a modest income in those days from printing and selling cloth, she ensured the kids regularly had little treats such as trips to the children's park. [12]

Music means so much to its lovers but hymns strengthen the faithful including its aged. The last time I saw Mrs. Kufuor in another hilarious mood was on her husband's December 8 birthday a couple of years back. She was being aided to her seat and for stability of movement, into their house's garden. The Winneba Youth Choir of which they serve as chief patrons had come to sing. As it would be on such occasions, the songs moved people who crowded the garden.

The English poet, William Cowper's, *Hark My Soul, It is the Lord* was particularly striking in sonority as she joined in the singing. Her joys showed in the layers of lyrical emotions between the verses:

Can a woman's tender care
Cease towards the child she bare?
Yes, she may forgetful be:
Yet will I remember thee.

*

Mine is an unchanging love,
Higher than the heights above,
Deeper than the depths beneath
Free and faithful, strong as death. [13]

Chapter Three

Faith and "The Testimonies of the Martyrs"

In March 2018, the University of Oxford Alumni Office decided it would be the sacred city of Rome or the 'external city' where it would gather its alumni, fellows and distinguished friends for its Meeting Minds. A biannual event, it gives alumni space to meet the famous and sages of the secular world. There are intellectual alignments from sciences to the revisionist treatise of great thinkers during such gatherings. Wines are from the best vineyards and dinners under great chandeliers popping decent conversations with running courses. It

Holy Mary and Intercession

Rome, Italy. The image of Mary the mother of Jesus is in Christian orthodoxy and among Catholics next in centrality to the son's. A plethora of art including of how an innocent Jewish village girl defied the expectations of a C1st Bethlehem. She is prayed to and could be divisive doctrinally. When in his last hours Jesus saw his mother, and the disciple (his cousin) John he said, "Woman, here is your son" and to John, "Here is your mother." From that time John "took her into his home." There was no instruction of inheritance. It was, many theologians say, his entrusting of her into the care of family and friends. The position of a Grotto of Mary in an Orthodox church yard could raise big issues. To the Pentecostal, charismatic and new founding churches of today, her elaborations are indeed limited.

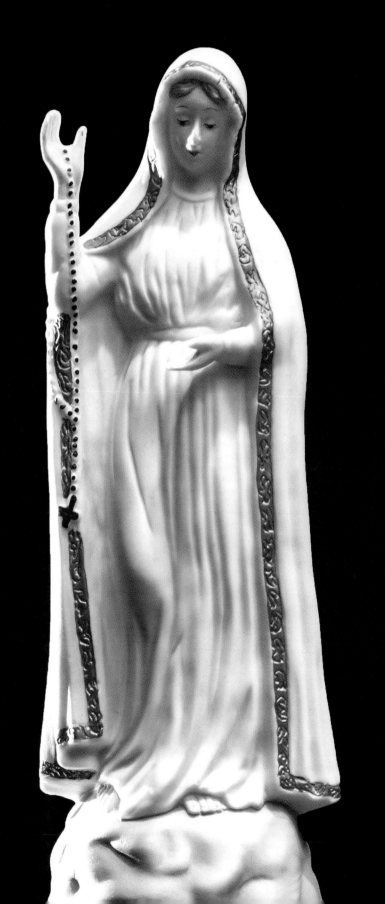

was typical in Rome. The University's Chancellor, Baron Patten of Barnes or better still, Chris Patten, the last British Governor of Hong Kong, one-time leader of the Conservative Party and chairman of the BBC Trust was among the major speakers.

Baron Patten's Catholic faith is fundamental to his being, he had publicly said. At one time, he was being consulted by the Vatican to help with reforms of its sclerotic civil structure and to create a more efficient bureaucracy. He is an example of faith, high indulgence in politics of consequence - power and glory that comes with it. Yet, his humility, as observed by close associates, is always around him. Rome, the external city has the elements of these too: its ancient politics was of intrigue under the imperial powers of emperors and how humble martyrs emerged out of it at the end.

Though I had previously visited it and the Vatican City, it brought a momentary indecision as to whether to go again, this visit was different. And the only unfulfilled part of the programme had to do with the group's inability to visit the Vatican Gardens which had been closed. Otherwise, the University with its network and alumni in sensitive and controlling positions globally, easily gets things done.

They made it up when an Indian nun of one of the higher Orders was given as our guide. It meant we had access to sensitive areas including the chapels, huge hanging art works and smelted ones that the curators of St. Peter's Basilica control. Galilee and East Jerusalem like Rome, share great monuments of the Christian faith but it is perhaps Rome and Italian artists particularly, sculptors and painters who immersed themselves; more than Jewish artists in faith art: chapel designs of the Basilica, the saints and their tombs and a panoramic pictorial passage. My reflections of that visit was more poetic - *Keeper of the Remains*:

On this Hill they paid the supreme price of faith.

Of faith shaken or semi-frozen.

But restored after the resurrection.

A time of revolutionary defiance in evangelism.

What power overcame them in this exercise of empire relations?

This empire of empires?

Rome as mosaic of future faith and civilisation?

This is a sacred Hill of martyrs.

Disciples:

Crucifixion of Peter upside down.

His remains the centrality of this great Basilica's dome.

Of Paul the philosopher's beheading.

The latter- day faith advocacy.

The abode of others unknown.

Two thousand is long in years.

Yet, the Hill stands in history.

The Carpenter's Son

Brazil. Christian or orthodoxy art centres around the birth and times of Jesus' mission. Rowan Williams the former Archbishop of Canterbury estimated that the mission lasted four years. The work of the apostles defined the second phase. Many nations, including the biggest in the world today, have been founded on the principles of The Trinity and large parts of European civilisations—from Greece, the United Kingdom before the unification, Spain, Italy, to France in particular, were touched by the carpenter's son.

On a State visit to Brazil, Kufuor, known to be Catholic, was presented with this marble art of Jesus manufactured in China.

What inspired the architecture of this site?

Went through the minds of the succession of architects?

Imitation of the crucifix for such creation?

This art story of antiquity is daily repetition.

Each time and day brings new revelations:

"The testimonies of the martyrs."

ii

Art is not for its sake.

The Passion story is the cumulative ministry of three to four years.

Its virtual interpretation the art of great Italian masters:

Michelangelo's and Leonardo's as forebears.

Through them we know:

Michelangelo's The Pieter- the Blessed Lady receives her dead son in her

arms.

The song of Good Friday - a transition of Lent to The Passion:

"Can a woman's tender care

Cease towards the child she bares?

Yes, she may forgetful be

Yet will I remember thee."

Or to the darker moment on the cross.

A Passion memorial:

"On Calvary's tree, he suffered for me

The just for the unjust that I might be free

His Grace is abundant, His Love is divine

Oh wonder of wonders, this saviour is mine."

iii

Saints adore the many chapels.

Incorporeal in their tombs but their stories the blocks of great faith.

The pilgrims surge forth and backwards,

of the world's many nationalities,

the force of the story becomes abundant.

The songs of regret lead to those of salvation: three days after.

Easter's tone is different: It could be the Tedium. [14]

∽❦⎯•∙●◑ ‖ ◐●∙•⎯❦∽

The Catholic Archbishop Emeritus of Kumasi, Peter K. Sarpong, also a distinguished social anthropologist, has delineated art as "dealing with human workmanship as opposed to the work of nature." [15] On material art like the ones I have written about here, he believes that they alone, like carving of wood or metal, whether for a crucifix, or a traditional stool, can enhance each other to ensure that there is full impact. He wrote about: "Literary art, such as a piece of poem, the art of statesmanship, namely skill in governing people, the art of diplomacy, that is the way we deal with people in delicate matters so that the intended effect is achieved without an offence being caused."[16]

Kufuor and Pontiff

Rome. Ghana. An Anglican convert to Catholicism, Kufuor met in the course of his presidency with Pope John Paul in 2002 and together with the King of Asante, Otumfuo Osei Tutu II, visited the Vatican on the invitation of Pope Francis in 2015.

Thus, faith depends on other forms of art to grow: the paintings of the Stations of the Cross or Way of Sorrows, in other words, the pathway of Jesus to his death - Via Dolorosa being material art, needs art management to get the intended effect. And inside the St. Peter's Basilica, you will alongside paintings, also read biblical poetry or the words of prophets as complementary. They may include, depending on one's reading, the diplomacy of the apostles when they were faced with challenges of life and death.

How does a politician like Baron Patten or more at home Kufuor, an Anglican convert to Catholicism combine art forms in power-play, distribution and more critically, what artistic images inspire his faith? He is a friend of Cardinal Peter Turkson, the first Ghanaian Cardinal at the Vatican and more than a friend to Archbishop Sarpong who counseled him as president and he revels. He met Pope John Paul in 2002 and Francis at the Vatican in 2015. The first as sitting president and the second as former president visiting with the King of Asante, Otumfuo Osei Tutu II.

"From the beginning of time", Kufuor explains, "institutions of power have seen totems or decorations of art as authority over other dominions. Anywhere you look, there are complex structures and inert palaces, weaponry, carriages, fabrics through human history." These had and still have deeper meaning. Whereas in the past they were exclusive and functionary he says, these representations are now for mass appreciation. "It is the attribute of power that could be said to have caused ancient monarchs like Solomon to build The Temple and the Pagodas of the Eastern civilisation to come into existence. Art broke the mystique of power." [17]

Chapter Four

Africa of Our Forebears

Africa as the origins of humanity is in less dispute. Evidence abounds from the southern part of the continent from great archeological support showing that millions of years back, there were human habitations through relics such as vases, pottery and other metals for domestic usage. Academics and geologists for ease of narration normally divide this 11.67 million square miles, the second largest after Asia, into four entities. The North which extends to the Sahara Desert passes through the Nile Valley. The fertility of this area goes further into the Mediterranean. [18]

⬟ Men and Women on Horseback

Sahel/West Africa. Horses have been a form of human and cargo transport in Africa's savannah. Influenced by Islam and ancient trade, they were and are also used by traditional kings and queens beyond their abode and internationally. On ceremonial occasions, you could, whether in Kano in northern Nigeria or Mali, see retinue of men on horseback at the end of Ramadan. They could be dressed in colours signifying the occasion and are trained to express joy and behave in mournful situations if need be.

This particular woman as I indicate in the text reminds one (not by way of military dress) of the Dahomey Amazons, the female warriors of the ancient Kingdom of Dahomey who were said to be terrible in battles against enemies as vanguards of the queens in the 1600s.

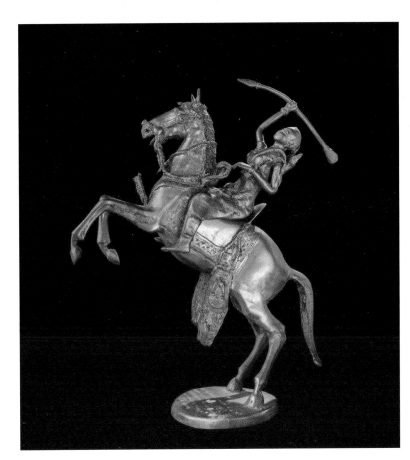

There is the East which is counted from northern Egypt, the Horn of Africa and is seen through the Great Lakes and as far as to Mozambique in the south. Some include with it the highlands of Ethiopia. Then there is Central Africa which lies in the equatorial rainfall belt side by side with the woodlands. The last of the South gets to the North through the Kalahari Desert which geographers equate to the long stone-age history. [19]

The powers of African cultures reinforce these 54 countries of over a billion people and with their thousands of languages. Its geographic histories of natural resources are abundant in the world. They include every hard and soft commodity in international trade of gold, silver, diamond, bauxite from the West coast - Ghana and Ivory Coast through Nigeria to the Democratic Republic of Congo. Congo's resources are so abundant that from the colonial aggression of Belgium, its brutal civil war of the Congo Crisis of the 1960s, its mineral resources are still under exploitation by outsiders including Africans. Its underdevelopment ironically is because of its wealth which should it be marshalled in conditions of order could supply the needs to most of Africa and beyond. Telecommunication technology which is fast changing the global market has its elements of manufacturing in the Congo.

Petroleum and oil discovery have always been part of Africa's geographic make-up. In the last decade and before, Ghana, Ivory Coast,

Uganda have discovered oil and are now oil economies. Soft commodities or what are called traditional exports such as cocoa, coffee, cashew, peanuts, cereals, cattle or livestock have been traded in for centuries.

When people talk about global markets and 21st century economics, it is about what we have seen or read about before. On March 21, 2020, it was reported by Africanews that of the over 90 million cattle reared in Chad, making thirty percent of its economy, an agreement had been signed between it and Angola for the former to supply 3,000 cattle on quarterly basis for a number of years to Angola. This would be in exchange for petroleum products and cash. With low foreign reserves and lower Gross Domestic Product and consequent per capita, this bilateral trade agreement is almost back to the old African trading system. Both had engaged in brutal wars - Islamic fundamentalism re-positioning in Chad and ideological socialist posturing of a still closed and oil export economy in Angola. Livestock farming is low due to climatic conditions and years of post-conflict adjustment in both cases. Meat products necessitate high import bills and state subsidy with an already low foreign reserves.

These economic and cultural livelihoods in parts of Africa were underpinned by systems of political governance in which traditional chieftaincy prevailed with hierarchical powers from the clan and

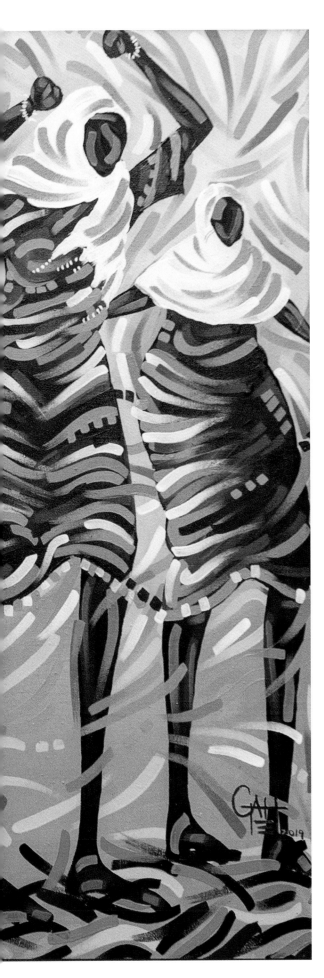

● Women of Ramadan

2019- Upper West. Four Muslim women engage in a possible Dagbani dance-form from the ancient Kingdom of Dagbon in northern Ghana. It is an Eid-al Adha or Festival of Sacrifice time which is the second holy holiday after the Ramadan. It is characterised with slaughtering of a cow, feast procession and hilarious attitudes by different social and cultural groups. This painting of women with Hijabs could also be of the Wa and the Wala, the Muslim ethnic group in the Upper West of Ghana who since the 17th century have been involved in international trade within the neighbourhood.

into high authority in which judiciary, legislative and executive powers were spread.

Like many in Europe and the Americas, societies in pre-medieval times had consolidated social and political capitals through war engagements in which the vanquished were incorporated into the victors'. The military structures developed by the Asante made it a great power in the 19th century. But there was no ethnic identity or people called Asante before then; it was war that brought them together against another imperial entity. Before Asante there were kingdoms in the northern Gold Coast colony and the Dagombas were a self-respecting political organisation with huge influence.

These also remind us that military leadership in West Africa was not male exclusive and that we had for instance, the Dahomey Amazons or Mino (Our Mothers), an ancient female army said to be five thousand strong, skilful and ferocious in battles who served as the body-guards of the queens of Dahomey, today's Republic of Benin. There were similar female armies in Somalia that repelled Islamic crusaders and Italian soldiers intended on colonisation as captured in paintings and in Mazrui's, *The Africans - A Triple Heritage*.

There is of course the supreme signature of nation-building and artistic development in Mali by its Emperor Sundiata who died in 1255. The art of Griots in West Africa, particularly The Epic of Sundiata is a moving epic poetry in African military history. The Lion of Mali or The Lion King as his appellations go, had advised that not only his achievements but the civilisation of Mali and Africa should reflect in these epics and that the world and posterity should know of them. The musical instruments developed for this including the Kora, the Khalam or Xalam have replicas made today for tourists and seen as art as are the paintings of the old cities of Gao, Timbuktu and the centres of learning he built which were continued by his nephew, Mansa Musa, one of the wealthiest kings the world ever knew. So sure was Sundiata of posterity's remembrance that when the United States' best known multimedia brand, The Walt Disney Company or Disney created the multiple award-winning animation, "The Lion King" to be followed by its musical, many historians pointed to Sundiata- the story of The King of Savannah or The Lion of Mali as influencing the production.

These centuries-old developments were however, first altered through internal conditions of military rivalry and economic advantages. There was however the external that came through continental and international influences: the spread of Christianity from Europe to the colonies of Africa, the Caribbean and Latin America and North America over a sustainable period from the crusaders.

The emergence of Islam from North Africa into Sub-Saharan Africa would not only change the socio-economic conditions and systems

Moonlight Stories

Sahel. Transmission of family histories, folklore stories and poetry in West Africa at the evening fire-side or in moonlight is ancient. The Kwaku Ananse stories in Ghana, the Yoruba Esu Elegbara, now one of the influential folklores in African-American's tradition of The Signifying Monkey are examples. In the Sahel, it comes after communal dinner in big bowls followed possibly by recitation of the Koran and Arabic classical compositions. In the sand deserts of Qatar or Dunes of Qatar in the south-west of the capital, Kufuor once spent hours with Arab friends and their families drinking fresh camel milk and a dinner of rice and camel stew under moonlight reflection from connecting deserts of Iran.

This is a pastoralist with a *burgami* (a Hausa name for a traditional water holder). It is normally made of the skin of cattle or sheep.

but affect growth: human and trade relations opened up and exchange of goods and services increased with new settlements and dual citizenship in some of their trading countries. In fact, some of the powerful kingdoms had resident diplomats- mastered in politics and trade negotiations based in the capitals.

For instance, Kwame Boatin, an envoy of the King of Ashanti spent years in the Dagomba Kingdom. There was an Ashanti royal who was given up in marriage to the Dagomba royalty as a sign of friendship. This was after Boatin was made part of the delegation to London to negotiate a peace agreement as the British were bent on incorporating Asante into its Gold Coast colony. The delegation was still in negotiation when Joseph Chamberlin ordered the invasion of Kumasi. Subsequently, King Prempeh and 54 others including Boatin were exiled to the Seychelles Islands from 1897. [20]

Long before Prempeh's exile for instance, Kumasi was a very cosmopolitan trade centre as it led not only to the northern parts of the Gold Coast but to the Upper Volta (today's Burkina Faso), Niger, Mali and other Sahelian regions like northern Nigeria and The Sudan. Nationals including from Sierra Leone, engaged in trading of all goods and were identified in some quarters of Kumasi. There were in some cases, intermarriages between the indigenes and these immigrants, some of whom were international currency dealers or money changers.

There are still some powerful resident Malians and French speaking Nigeriens in the informal currency exchange business of the Economic Community of West African States and other major European currencies; with enough monetary power, they sometimes determine the daily exchange rate based on demand and supply, and suppression of currency circulation. Again, many of the livestock imports, cultural products such as carpets, leather furniture of animal skins, foot-rest, baskets and bags into southern Ghana from its north and its neighbourhood are by these kindred merchants.

Kufuor remembers that when growing up in Apagyafie near the palace in the mid 1940s, there were many of these traders around the neighbourhood who sold goods to households. On a three-day visit to Mali as President in December 2006, he was extremely shocked when he met the Ghanaian community traders and among them Malians who had lived in his Kumasi neighbourhood. The elderly knew his mother and family. In fact, they spoke to him in Twi, his mother tongue. And he realised that these former sojourners saw themselves as cosmopolitans. Some of their architectural designs were obviously influenced by their times in Kumasi.

Governance systems and the three elements of production - land tenure, capital and labour, property ownership and assets would all change by these interventions of travels and knowledge. Some were

Man With A Game

Sahel. Hunting and gathering had been ancient means of food and meat supplies in households. Hunters were most of the time also farmers. They are different from herdsmen or pastoralists, in the sense that the latter rear livestock as full occupation and are in control of their commercial potential.

⬟ A Water Supplier

Mali/Sahel. West Africa's nomadic culture has been part of the agricultural ecosystem for centuries. This metal sculpture of a Nigerien herdsman has two buckets on a metal support from water wells. With a neck talisman against presumed evil protection, a broad hat for head and body against hot temperature, there had been intermittent clashes, property destruction and death with competing farmers for land as water bodies get contaminated by grazing cattle. Whether from Niger, Burkina Faso or Kano, ECOWAS protocols of free movement of persons, residence or transhumance fruitlessly prevented clashes.

⬟ Banana Farm

2015 - Ghana. A foliage of agriculture. A banana farm plantation with a top-left farm house built of brick and decaying palm roof. It also has an irrigation stream at a possible harvest time sale. Some bananas are already packed in crates by two women whilst other wholesale operatives await their supplies. For centuries in West African agrarian economies, apart from transportation of foodstuffs from the hinterlands by male cargo drivers, women have dominated the sector as farmers and market guilds including in price determination.

unavoidable as they were impositions whether through Slave Trade, Colonial rule or its post-colonial.

These situations were captured in art manifested in many museums across Africa by explorers or commissioned voyagers on assignment from European monarchies before the medieval period. The decision by the Government of Belgium in 2019 to return some artefacts to the Congo and the building of a museum to showcase its collection of mostly Congolese art is indicative.

When Kufuor became President of Ghana in 2000, he had a consciousness of both the past, which should be known because it was rich with systems, and the present because it could be explained by the past. At one point he reviewed his own positions on both when speaking on, Leadership, Government and Entrepreneurship in Africa:

i. Excepting its Mediterranean northern lands, Africa remained outside the routes of the ancient trading, cultural and imperial hegemonistic interactions that engendered and evolved the various Asian and European civilisations. The forbidding Sahara Desert immediately South of North Africa effectively cut most of the continent off till about the 10th century A.D.

ii. When the venturesome Latins, chiefly the Portuguese and Spanish, eventually sailed down the Atlantic Ocean in the

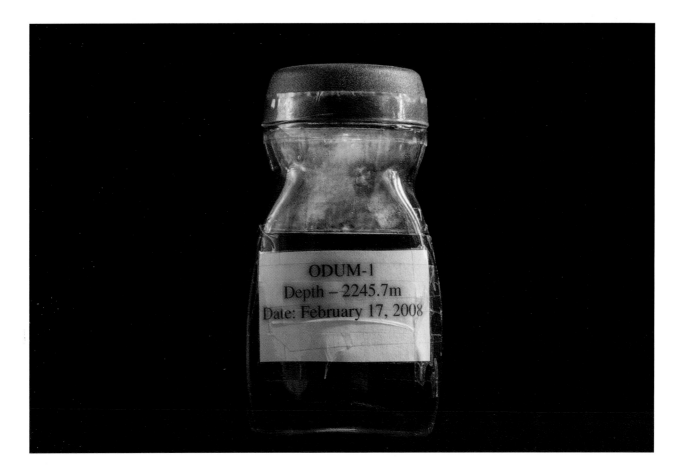

⬠ Oil Discovery

2007- Ghana. Odum - 1, Depth - 2245.7m, February 17 2008. In 2007, Ghana discovered oil in commercial quantity as it was celebrating its fiftieth anniversary from colonial rule. The field of discovery, appropriately named Jubilee Field was among others that the US Kosmos Energy worked on. In this bottle is the first drip of the oil presented to Kufuor. Since then, there have been further discoveries in Ghana and parts of Africa.

14th century, the rest of the continent, mainly Africa South of the Sahara, came under the long onslaught of the debilitating Slave Trade and later colonialism. This period lasted for almost six hundred years. The intercourse Africa South of the Sahara was forced into with the marauding Europeans, was more or less a one-sided institutionalised gang RAPE and highly exploitative. This continued till Ghana gained independence in 1957. The rest of the African nations followed and South Africa brought up the rear with the collapse of the evil Apartheid system in 1994. [21]

Thus, international agreements have had prototypes in old bilateral systems. Mostly informal, it is still the case with low trade infrastructure on the continent. It had been some of these trade instincts from peasants or the so-called primary producers who ensured that post-harvest losses were arrested. In 2018, plantain farmers in the Ashanti-Akyem district developed a strategy that also ensured that excess plantain and other crops would not rot against their labour and capital. Of Government's inability to purchase, or absence of a commodity exchange, they discovered a huge deficit of supply and market and therefore mobilised their surplus production, arranged with truck and cargo companies, found French-speaking interpreters and were able to sell in Burkina Faso, re-creating the ancient trading routes.

Chapter Five

Between South of the Orient and Occident is Our Abode

China's emergence as a global power in the C21st has only been a prototype of its ancient recovery. The Song Period or era of its history saw the most amazing flourish in arts and culture, particularly in ceramics - the manufacturing of vases and pottery, which were found in the homes of emperors, kings and queens and of the aristocracy. Ceramics and architectural designs had exotic influences in

Pottery as Evidence

2013 - Galilee and (2019)-Kumasi. One finding which traverses civilisations in the work of archeologists is pottery. They may come or be found in different soil types and geographic locations but it has often been evidence of human habitation, as domestic utility: water storage, cooking utensil or plate. With these two pots, it becomes difficult to know which comes from where without an explanation. Both were bought by the author. The smaller one in Cana in Galilee where Jesus turned water into wine - his first miracle and the other, from a craftsman in Accra possibly from Pankorono near Kumasi.

the Ottoman period in the Middle East, and in Europe among the Greeks, Romans and the British in particular. These elicited interest in great institutions in Europe including Oxford, Cambridge and later, the School of Oriental and African Studies in Sinology. They have some of the best expertise on Chinese and East Asian cultures: from music, manufacturing of musical instruments to poetry and theatre architecture. The collections of Sinologists (including of Joseph Needham's) at these institutions are classical documentations.

The monarchical innovation and development of its meritocratic civil service could only be upwardly mobile. That period registered one of the highest economic and cultural growths the world has ever known. The refrain of the French warrior, Napoleon that China was a sleeping giant and that its awakening would shake the world might have begun in 1978 with Deng Xiaoping's reforms in the communist state. It was a complete change from the period of Mao and his variant of communism practice.

Communism might have taken sway over East Asia and in particular Taiwan (which was established after the communists took over China in 1949), Hong Kong, Malaysia and Singapore which carried mainly Chinese cultural traits and shared ancestry. The Cold War, consolidated statehood depending on which side one belonged to with post-World War geo-politics bringing its realignment, but Chinese cultural veins prevailed at the end.

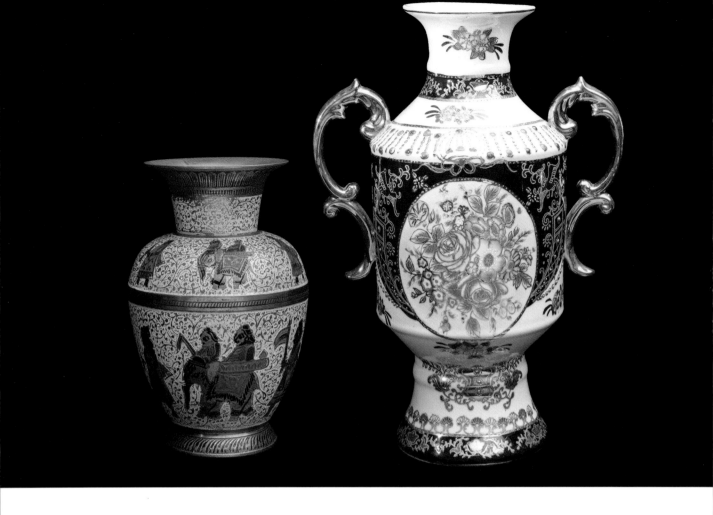

⬟ Vases from the East

China. The Song Period was the height of Chinese cultural flourish; in ceramics, terracotta design and classical art which would influence East and South-east Asia including Singapore, Malaysia, Hong Kong and Taiwan. It is sometimes difficult to differentiate between vases like these two from China and the smaller Korean one. They are reminders of their evolution. Kufuor had art gifts from both countries with their non-translations as the Chinese particularly do, of the ancient past from which they are emerging as a great global power in the C21st.

By the 1960s, China's relations with Ghana and other developing countries, were high and Nkrumah's visit to Eastern Europe in 1961 cemented his socialist orientation. It was also after his overthrow and the coming in of the Second Republic that, Kufuor as Deputy Minister of Foreign Affairs, voted for the One China Policy on behalf of the Progress Party Government at the United Nations.

Since that time, China-Africa relations has institutionalised not only with the assemblages of African leaders' multilateral attempt through the China-Africa Forum for Cooperation in trade, loans and grants but, also with infrastructure based development. From coast to coast in Africa, are Chinese machinery, engineers and sometimes labour, particularly from around 2005. Their imports have displaced trade with Europe, not to talk of intra-Africa trade.

In arts and culture, they have built national theatres and where possible, affiliation with universities of Confucius Institutions, after the great Chinese philosopher who though popular today had his descendants hounded out of China and parts of East Asia into exile during Mao's time.

Despite Japan's attempted colonisation of China, South Korea and others in its greater East Asia prosperity policy, the cultural basis of China and Korea in language development were too advanced to be corrupted or subsumed. Artistic elements, whether paintings of the

Great Wall or the military architectures are things they give out as gifts. That culture prevails in South Korea as well as in Singapore. In any case, it is sometimes very difficult to say (if not landmark buildings) whether what you have is from the mainland or from Singapore. Malaysia's Islamic culture could differentiate art work from its Chinese heritage somehow but, the latter's dominance is there in the East.

Into the third decade of the 21st century however, it had ceased to be just the East but the world. The projection of China as the biggest economy surpassing the United States would not be long in coming according to 'super forecasters.' Already, it leads with certain economic indicators.

Before the Korean War, it combined an oriental heritage which had suffered multiple invasions. Its great detest of Japan after the episode of the Comfort Women - the raping of Korean women by Japanese soldiers, would only mar their international relationship. Its closeness to China has to do with their near joint colonisation. That cultural bond had some level of influence in Korea's own art landscape especially in ceramics and cuisine. It is however, also undisputed that the Miracle on the Han River, which marks South Korea's transition to a modern economy and the agricultural policies reflected in the 1970s' infrastructure common fund, the Saemaul Undong, was with enormous aid assistance from the West, especially the United States during the Cold War. Its marine culture and development around

⬟ Iranian Vase

Iran. In its heydays as a great imperial power, Iran's Persia civilisation dazzled the world in the Middle East and beyond. Its military strength led to the conquest of neighbours including the Babylonian exile when the Jews were demanded to sing 'the Lord's songs in a strange land'. It is also reflected in science, petroleum wealth, Islamic power and in particular intricate designs of such art.

This vase with its saucer was a present from official Iranian diplomacy.

⬟ Of the Maghreb

2010 - Morocco. It is Islamic and this vase and saucer from Morocco is an example of its industrial complex. Islam developed fast from North Africa into its Saharan parts influencing the indigenous cultures of the Maghreb region and beyond. Through that and the Arabic language, indigenous cultures changed in Egypt for example (and later on The Sudan) and had to do with the use of Arabic, which affected the arts and the educational system.

A Bamboo Vase

2009- Accra. A little bamboo vase well treated and given colour by a Ghanaian craftsman in Accra. It has little utility value and this could be classified by some as decorative art. Craftsmen everywhere are influenced by what they see and like.

⬠ Garden Pot

2010- Accra. The utility or functional value of an item of art could have aesthetic dimensions. This garden pot is made of wood and ceramic material and has a frontal portrait of Kufuor and an adjacent colour embossment of Ghana's Coat of Arms originally designed in March 1957. It has four main quarters and other features. Quarter one of a sword and a staff for traditional governance, the second of Osu Castle which was once a colonial trade and administrative office, the third of Cacao tree depicting the agrarian nature of the old and new economies and the last of the goldfields. The artist situated Kufuor's portrait with these elements of power and even when he had retired from them, there is still the historical reference.

⬟ The Divine Bell of King Songdok the Great

2010 - South Korea. This is a replica bronze art of The Divine Bell of King Songdok the Great of Korea. A bronze made in 771AD, it is a precious treasure with simple calligraphy. Its modern and better known equivalent in concept and thought is the Peace Bell of Japan given to the UN in 1954.

Korean Woman

2010 - South Korea. Ceremonial Korean or traditional dress for women like the Hanbok are very elaborate. This full length ceramic portrait is more a composition of dress and deep expression apart from showing the features of a beautiful woman. Kufuor visited Korea as president and after, including when he was part of the policy preparatory and advocacy team when the country hosted the 5th G-20 Summit in 2010. He also received an honorary doctorate degree from a Korean University in 2011 for his leadership in Ghana and Africa.

the Korean Peninsula and technical assistance, would lead to the biggest ship manufacturing base in the whole of Asia and much of the world. It would affect the image and thinking of its artists.

'Modern' people, whether in China or Korea, like everywhere else tend to be less interested in heritage art and more consumed with 'global art.' When this happens, it is not the art, whether classical music, a piece of painting or a photography that is not appreciated; it is the artists and how they project these. According to the Artistic Director of the Carnegie Hall, formerly Managing Director of the London Symphony Orchestra, Sir Clive Gillinson, it's not market research that is needed to determine what people want to see, in which sense, it becomes predictable, but rather it should be from the artist's perspective of what they have to see.

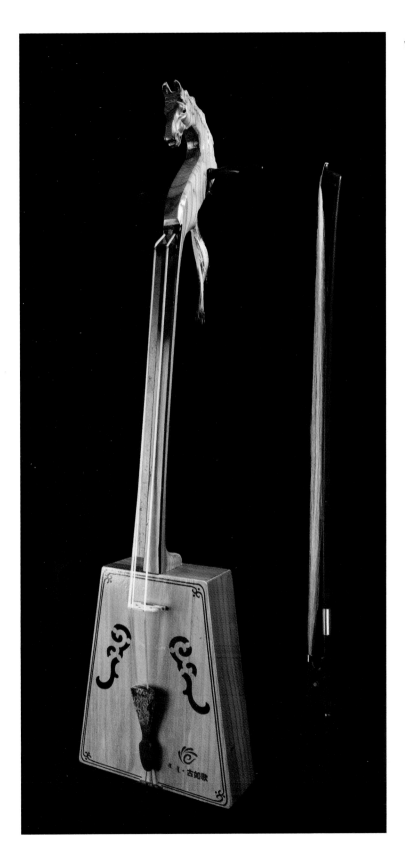

Violin of Inner Mongolia

Inner Mongolia. This violin instrument is from Mongolia, an autonomous part of Northern China which is still ethnically Chinese. The upper end is a sea-horse head sculpture piece depicting Mongolia as one of the geographic areas in Asia with a large sea-horse population.

Chapter Six

Before the Better Angels of Our Nature

The earth is God's nature. Humanity thrives for now but at least with limitation of science over nature. Without the nature of earth, we extinct and are pre-historic. But it is not just the earth but humanity's interaction with it that counts: we, the living and the highest order of animals like the lesser creatures, depend on it to reproduce, engage in science and technology inventions, to commune with God for the religious, and for survival of agricultural purposes - the land and its inherent soil, the weather, the climate and for which Christians at harvest time sing – "All Good Gifts Around Us are sent from heaven above". But liberty of the earth's utilisation has its ugly abuses of destruction of the ecosystem: the interest of humanity over other inanimate or less assertive natural members - of plants, animals, science and technology application and resultant crisis of climate change through pollution and death.

At old age, the earth beckons us, or when we die of self-inflicted diseases or of natural causes, it is in its belly we get buried. Notwithstanding its receptiveness as part of the cosmology, it is not detached. The sky above overshadows its existence daily through sunrise and set-down. The rains that nourish our beings and the solar energy with which we today produce electricity, are all good things from above. It is these factual observations and beliefs that, perhaps also influenced the Francophone Ivorian architect and poet, Joseph Miezan Bognini in *Earth and Sky:*

> *Earth and sky are infinities*
> *Where our cries cannot venture*
> *I have fixed my head between two stones*
> *Seeking the Shelterer in vain.*
> *Only your splendor sets me free*
> *I have run through the void*
> *Crossing a thousand villages*
> *Where could I draw breath*

Without damaging your scenery?

The nights have flayed me

Like a careless wanderer.

I am simply an insect

Without wings or paws

Scornful serpents are my only fare

Heat crackles upon my roof

The ripe fruit of my flesh is shrinking

Love lies crumpled at my feet.

I would strip myself of all my cares

And wear the dress of consolation only.

Such joy is new to me.

I will take you for my companion

My body is lost in your arms.

But make me insensate as the wind

Which smiles and ravages nature,

Not to make me hate you

But to love you always. [22]

⬟ Pavement Market

2019 - James Town, Accra. From the author's
young artist James Mishio who lives in Accra;
created and purchased in 2019. It's a panoramic
touch on colonialism and mobility in an informal
market. It inspired the poem, *Pavement Market*.
A painting very representative of African urban
markets and movement of goods. Without being told that this is of James Town, central Accra,
it will be difficult to know.

⬟ Market Street

2015-Kumasi. A market street painting by a visual artist, Bernard Mensah before he left Kumasi to the United States to practice and to design cloths. This is different from the *Pavement Market*. A somehow populated space, it has uneven high-rise architectures; a mosque in sight which is suggestive of patronage by the faithful or a Muslim community. Such a composite design is called a lane in Ghana:

Zongo Lane in Accra or Paul Sagoe Lane in Kumasi. But pavement markets are normally unautho-rised spaces and different from Market Day or temporary trading which could be once a week and urban driven from the outskirts and villages. It is also different from a market street with semi-per-manent or permanent status for trading such as, this sunset evening trading.

From creation, earthly violence by mankind and against other na-
tures, have led to wars: of religion and state control. The spread of
Christianity and Islam even as they had messages of peace and good-
will towards men, brought great crusades of human slaughter to regions of the world that before their arrivals had their own histories of
human destruction. And so the fountains – founders of these peace-
ful religions died through violence on earth.

Artists since creation, have had visual images and through literary
arts, of such stages of destruction. The ancient poets of Palestine
were considered prophets and in the Palestinian-Israeli conflicts that
intensified after 1948, citizens of both sides depended on their artists to interpret their anguish. When the Palestinian poet, Mahmoud
Darwish died and was to be buried in Ramallah, a fellow Palestinian
poet, Mourid Barghouti wrote that, "thousands of Palestinians with
poems and roses in their hands, went out to honour a poet whose
lines are full of butterflies, doves, bees, ancient mythology and biblical allusion." [23]

For Barghouti, this conflict of centuries, has led to destruction in
the world; to great terrorism upheavals, sometimes intangible to humanity. He wrote again: "All conflicts prefer symbols. Jerusalem is
the Jerusalem of theology. The world is concerned with the "status"

of Jerusalem, the idea and the myth of Jerusalem, but our lives in Jerusalem and the Jerusalem of our lives do not concern it. The Jerusalem of the sky will live forever, but our life in it is threatened with extinction."[24]

The Israeli or the Jewish novelist, Amos Oz who was liberal in thoughts and supported a two-state solution felt that, humanity also gets into conflict beyond the immediate interest of the protagonists. Europe and the European experience threatened the Jews perhaps far more. The Jews, he said, "were kicked out of Europe, my parents were virtually kicked out of Europe some seventy years ago, just like the Palestinians and then out of the Arab countries. When my father was a little boy in Poland, the streets of Europe were covered with graffiti, "Jews, go back to Palestine," or sometimes worse: "Dirty yids, piss off to Palestine." [25]

◦◦◦ ‖‖‖ ◦◦◦

The ugly and long historical nature if we leave the Middle East into Africa, is the same struggle of survival for space, leadership and human cooperation. In 2010, Kufuor was invited by the Interpeace, a Geneva-based peace-building alliance operating in over twenty countries including the Middle East and Palestine and in Africa, Rwanda and Liberia, to serve as Chair of its Governing Council. He replaced the Nobel laureate and former President of Finland, Martti

Ahtisaari. He was also concurrently Ambassador of the World Food Programme. His skills as negotiator in Liberia, Ivory Coast, Kenya and elsewhere, had taken him to these post-conflict programmes where fundamental economic and political orders were in disarray. Working with international non-governmental organisations could be more of advocacy of perceived goodness and the interest of the donors.

He also travelled through the continent especially in Ethiopia and Kenya and their rural parts, on issues to do with agricultural productivity and cultural practices inhibiting growth in East Africa among the Maasai areas, food distribution and its politics in famished communities. Kufuor's interest in agriculture when president, yielded positive results. Growth in traditional exports of cocoa was from 300,000 tons to close to a million; syndicated commodity loans were secured with local and international investment banks with lots of incentives given cocoa and commodity farmers. Similar programmes were developed for the blue economy on the coast.

This was linked to education and a School Feeding Programme. It was to ensure that there were sufficient free and compulsory enrolments in schools for infants. The concept of the School Feeding Programme, was also to prevent the perennial post-harvest losses as the educational districts were to ensure that food produced were purchased and that children were fed free of charge for at least once

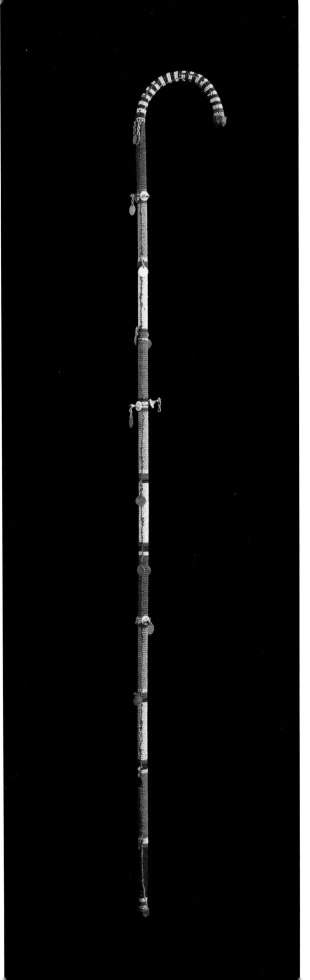

◗ Colours of the Maasai

2010 - Kenya. One of the early
international engagements Kufuor
had after his presidency was as an
Ambassador of the World Food
Programme. An assignment took
him to the very heart of the *Maasai*
habitation and raw cultural manners
in rural Kenya. It's become almost
impossible for some of them to have
or adapt to other forms of livelihoods aside their nomadic existence
and craftsmanship of rural and these
days, urban art. They are sometimes
at the mercy of international food
donors and government when there
is famine or the savannah eats into
their lands. After a long advocacy for
change, they gave him this walking
stick as a gesture.

Camel: Desert Transportation

Sahel. The life expectation of a camel is roughly 70 years. As desert transport for long distance because of its biological food storage, it had been part of the Mediterranean war histories and cultures. Wealth could be calculated on camel possessions. Its body products are for domestic consumption as meat, milk for beverages including export and for manufacturing of industrial products. Its cultural significance in marriage and family continuity is structured across cultures whether in Qatar or Iran.

a day. With food security assured, together with free transport for school kids and other programmes with the multilateral institutions such as the World Bank and the International Monetary Fund, money was freed to further social intervention measures such as water treatment and supply.

Non-industrial scale agriculture - still rain-fed, climate change and its effect on planting and harvesting, and of yields are unpredictable. If water for agriculture is a big issue, water for domestic and industrial usage is as well. If you visit Nima in Accra, the country's biggest underclass or shark populated area (like Alexandria Town in Johannesburg or the terrible livelihood of Soweto or Kabila in Kenya), you will find resident-immigrants from Niger, Burkina Faso and Mali with Fulani roots and cultural lingua Franca of Hausa. They still have wells and fetch water from them as is the practice in parts of the Sahel region.

Market infrastructure in major Ghanaian cities particularly in Accra, Kumasi but also in Koforidua, had been expanded through these social intervention programmes of the 2000s. The aim was to decrease the growing informal and pavement markets which are visible in major African cities with the same attitudes.

The Elephant - Osono

Ghana and East Africa. Significant animals, by way of size, wits, or features, have stories or proverbs framed around them. *Esono akyiri nni aboa*- There is no animal of equal size as the elephant or "After the elephant there is no other animal." [42] This proverb was developed into a war song projecting one's military might and strategy, by the Akan. It is the symbol of the New Patriotic Party to which Kufuor belongs. Of all his collections, right from the door into his living room, are the art gifts of elephants of all sizes and media - wooden, metal and ceramic. Political adherents say its meat or carcass is big enough, figuratively to serve a nation if equitably distributed. It is a participatory animal. To tourists however, it is one to be seen. They travel to the northern part of Ghana or to Botswana which has one of the world's largest elephant populations. With sunrise, elephants trek to water pond sites within the forest and could be very dangerous to sensors of threat or poaching. Though outlawed in South Africa and Kenya, poaching is sometimes allowed in Botswana to reduce overpopulation.

⬟ Giraffe

Kenya. Giraffes are an endangered mammal species at the verge of extinction. Global population is a little over 100,000. The Africa Wildlife Foundation says that apart from Kenya and a couple of other countries, they are fewer now. Man's use of land including for large-scale agriculture, industrial expansion, certain cultural practices including animal trading and food cultures account for this. Environmental activists campaign against their poaching and certain human practices, otherwise they say, their extinction will be an unfortunate occurrence. Sculpture pieces like this will be a reminder of once a living mammal.

In poetics, *Pavement Market*, a work bought from my regular art vendor more than explains such a market scene:

The market is unstructured.
Over-populated traders take over the twin-long but parallel pavements.
The street, an island for vehicular motion is even a shared-space:
busy pedestrians avoid the patches of pot-holes as the drivers do;
drivers of colonial cargo vehicles - Mammy Wagons with slow accelera-
tion but some reassuring inscriptions:
We will survive.
Pedestrians disregard red-traffic lights
and drivers honk and honk in protest.
They return insults with profane and abusive words.
Truck-pushers struggle with over-load on this street-island.
In competition with mobile hawkers:
shouting their wares for sale - dog chains, some stolen mobile phones,
second-hand clothing.
But some are wolf-criminals; surveyors of pedestrians' wallets,
of the villagers in city.
It's a survival for space.
Life of many hustles.
Nothing is calm except the stationary female hawkers:
wooden small tables form long columns, dozens of arranged tomatoes,
onions, fruits.

In rough trading gears and trousers;

their beauty somehow mingled with this.

They search for daily bread.

As against infringement of city planning and congestion rules.

Unabated is the endless fights with revenue collectors.

Because:

they hawk,

but fulfil income tax obligation.

A disconcerted lot;

in shelter colonial buildings of past grace.

That is before:

the pre-missing wooden windows, thirst of paint, of regeneration of fall-

ing concrete blocks and mortar disintegration.

Once beautiful, their secondary purpose now is:

refugee for the unsettled, commodity queens, hawkers of petty urban

trading. [26]

IV

International organisations that recognised Kufuor's agriculture and food security efforts, included the United States' State Department and in 2011, Hilary Clinton as Secretary of State announced that Kufuor and the President of Brazil, Lula da Silva had been awarded the World Food Prize. The formal presentation in Iowa was preceded by powerful speeches from the winners and the citation had everything to do with food as a basic element of human survival.

Kufuor's interest in farming is a family story. His uncles had created huge wealth in Kumasi and inherited thousands of acreage of land as cocoa farmers and merchants dealing with transnational corporations. With some of this wealth converted into other assets, his generation of what was an extended one, also had good education locally and internationally, before they assumed public and international roles.

After his presidency, he established in Daban, the home of his ancestors, a 100-acre cocoa farm with its house, cultivated other crops including orange and employed a staff of about 100. It's a legacy farm that would have an estate within the deep forest, an airstrip and a mountainous residential enclave. It is also to encourage the upcoming generation not to see farming as a rural occupation or as one for the uneducated.

If the better angels of our nature is service to humanity, or to one another, the artist sometimes serves as the visual and non-visual preserver of all.

Chapter Seven

Ethnography of Art and Cosmopolitan Aspirations

British colonial policies, with respect to cultures and ethnographic art, were most interesting. In West Africa from the mid-1800s, and apart from political control of traditional systems, iconoclasm and philistinism, were sometimes used as tools of policy implementation. The destruction and looting of The Aban in Kumasi in 1874 was repeated in The Kingdom of Benin among the Edo people in 1897.

In both cases, there was no excessive resistance to British request of access or political control. Huge differences in understanding of customary practices and disrespect for traditional African values and authority, were the immediate causes. The 1900 last Anglo-Ashanti war, was premeditated even as negotiations were ongoing. The killing of British army officers in Edo when the Oba of Benin requested them not to visit the kingdom, that is, during a time of religious curfew, were disobediences that served as immediate cause for the war and looting of thousands of Benin bronze and brass works. [27]

The looting of the Benin art was defining in many respects. The intricate portraits had always been under the palace's control and craftsmen were full-time professionals of copyrighted works and their raw materials. Art was not meant as a commercial engagement here or in some of the big kingdoms in West Africa. The king of Asante as a typical example, had always had copyright to certain kente designs and created a chief who was responsible for his kente weaving. So, the chief of his clothes at the palace - Abenasehene was the liaison with Bonwire, the town not far from Kumasi where weaving had been for over 300 years.

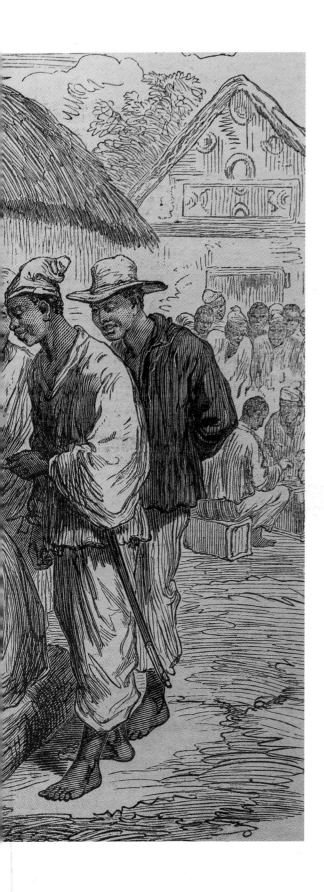

⬟ Recreation

1874 - Ashanti. The native soldiers of Ashanti as the British war reports described them, are seen here playing Oware, a C17th game in what is obviously a posed situation for the artist. It is very irregular to get fourteen spectators for the game. The British soldier in helmet on the left might have commandeered them to do so with smiling faces. It's even hard for some to see the game marbles. They are also in different clothes and hats in their contemplation - some Yoruba-looking ones and of the two players more or less in Islamic dresses. The British sometimes had military enforcement from other West African colonies in dealing with the Ashanti. If we look at the right of the main painting, there is a similar if not a replication, of the game play. One wonders what the British soldiers on the far left were in attention for if not a social curfew with their presence.

The only good thing that came from the Benin looting was that, when the art works got to Britain and other parts of Europe, it generated shock of the glorious art of an underestimated people. A Eurocentric explanation that it could have been as a result of possible contact with Europeans or those of a higher civilisation did not register. If, as some art historians argue, the people of Benin might have been influenced by the Yoruba from Ife, it still does not diminish its West African origins. It is difficult to know of the art works taken from the palace, as apart from thousands kept at museums, especially The British Museum and other European ones, many more were sold to private collectors.

In the case of Asante and in, *A Catalogue of Ashanti Art taken from Kumasi in the Anglo-Ashanti War of 1874,* the items and their histories make over 600 pages. [28] The looting in Benin became world famous and that shows the extent to which it is difficult to know the numbers. Of course, the origins of many of these art works and their makers at the time were known by the British or French colonial administrators. The ethnic groups had not by policy been assimilated completely and so some idiosyncrasies prevailed.

When that phase of creative doubt passed with acknowledgement of these art works, there was the great cultural mobilisation. The European powers still saw a greater value of cultural economy even as they despised these cultures. The first World War had weakened their economies, influence and prestige. It would partly be the same colonies that would be used to revive them. And so in 1924, King George V opened what became known as The British Empire Exhibition in 1925. It brought 56 former colonies to Wembley Park and was said to be the biggest exhibition the world or Britain had ever organised. [29]

Turn-outs of both European and international participants including Africans, were 27 million people. The reason for the exhibition was mainly economic: "to stimulate trade, strengthen bonds and bind mother country to her sister states and daughters, to bring into closer contact the one with each other, to enable all who owe allegiance to the British flag to meet on common ground and learn to know each other." [30] Great planning had gone into this - of the architecture of the Park (which would later become the Wembley Stadium) and the planning that involved visual artists, poets and novelists including, the detective one - Agatha Christie and her husband. [31]

Forty solid years after this great event, the British establishment knew its limitation in the emerging global economy after World War II. Its power had been further eroded and the importance of markets and numbers were of essence to talented politicians and economists which included the great one, John Maynard Keynes. Independence eventually came to the colonies but the British had the idea also of the Commonwealth of Nations which had everything to do with cultures, markets and economies.

⬟ Diplomacy of Divide and Rule.

1895- Ashanti. Two British senior diplomats on a visit to Kumasi. With a Fanti interpreter (in white cloth and jumper and a top-hat) they meet with chiefs in what is described as a friendly discussion. It is likely that in this November 30, 1895 painting were chiefs or royals who later supported the British deportation of Nana Agyeman Prempeh to the Seychelles Islands. After the 1900 War, some became pro-British. Not being royals but dissidents, they were elevated to undeserved traditional political positions.

The Commonwealth, headed by Queen Elizabeth II decided that by 1965, there should be another cultural festival with the colonies. The generation that attended this one were mostly not born or were not part of the Wembley Exhibition but they ("from the Indian sub-continent to the Antarctic ends of Australasia') also spoke of its great organisation and intensity. They included African playwrights, visual artists and poets, one of whom wrote:

119

> The Commonwealth Arts festival, 1965, was a child of the Independence "Wind of Change". One after the other, the colonies loosed the sash that bound them to the "great White Mother", bouncing like precious children into the modern world. The GWM however was not about to let them go off in their own independent directions. Commercial enticements were strengthening, mutual Defense Pacts furtively inserted into protocols…. It was a grand festival, the equal of which - except that it was also a lesson in cultural variety and organisation - would not be attempted (to the best of my knowledge) until the Negro Arts Festival in Dakar. [32]

Participants, whether producers of rustic handicraft or pottery, from Ife or Cape Coast or among the Shona, were seen as ethnographic artists with specific influenced art. But on the international stage, their identities had changed to be Nigerians, Ghanaians, Zimbabweans because they had participated from nations of the Commonwealth and their selection, most likely based on artistic creation and not ethnography.

That transition had in fact been part of the pre-Independence debate - how do the many cultures become national without some losing out? How does a nation of seventy ethnic groups with cultural diversities, become one? If colonialism was good for anything, it was to give a platform for such foliage. Kwame Nkrumah was all out to use these diversities for a national one and eventually, a Pan African personality but sooner than later, he realised the difficulties.

So, whilst Independence geared towards greater and global exposure and fulfilment of ambition and markets, there was a point at which other influences came to bear. It could have been through mostly education in Europe and a lot of those who showed promise and were excellent artists, did go. Some of these influences were dictated by international markets and indulgences.

In the last half century, this might have changed artistic creations and techniques but the artists made their names from the creativity around them. When Soyinka won the Nobel Prize, the citation mentioned the art and traditions of his Yoruba people. When Chigozie Obioma published, *The Fishermen* which story is set in Akure in Southwestern Nigeria and which does not even set itself in Lagos, it became an international best-seller and easily translated into over thirty languages.

The products from Africa at Sotheby's, Christie's and Tate are of settings or images of the continent. It shows there is within cosmopolitanism, elements or parts of small and big geographic imaginations which make it and without which, it does not exist. In that sense, Peggy Appiah's Ashanti gold-weights collection, could be global and cosmopolitan but at the same time, ethnographic.

It also means that generations of Africans can use Africa as a base to add or subtract for a purpose. When the Commonwealth itself evolved, its church services or faith gatherings at London's Westminster Abbey were Anglican-biased. Increasingly, and to make it more reflective of the cultures of its thirty percent global population, they became reflective of its diversity.

At one of such events broadcast to the world from London, was a choreography of music and dance. A particular dance was seemingly Central African with its jumping to the beat of whistles and geometric movements. I was very surprised when the television commentator said it was Ghanaian. There was obviously in my thought, no major dance form from Ghana that combined so many forms and with less identifiable costume. However, the Ghanaian choreographer had merged dance forms of Africa and the Caribbean. His appeal was to a broader Commonwealth audience.

⬠ Tribal Art of Xhosa

2006 - South Africa. Tribal Africa in South Africa is a well-known art manufacturing company for creation of figurines using local materials for distinguished personalities and rural lives. In this particular one, it is "a cluster of related tribes living in the Transkei district of the Cape Province. The Transkei is bordered on the east by the magnificent wild coast on the Indian Ocean and on the west by the majestic mountains of Lesotho. The tribes vary a little in dress, each picturesque in the blankets, gleaming brass and colourful bead necklaces.

Nelson Mandela was a Xhosa. These exquisite figurines are hand-made by the local people in Knysna on South Africa southern Cape Town. Each figure is individually made piece by piece including the decorating and finishing."

TRiBAL AFRICA

KNYSNA SOUTH AFRICA

In any case, it should not have surprised me. In 1998, I was an advisor to the musical theatre production - *Yaa Asantewaa Warrior Queen* funded by the Arts Council of England with almost $2 million. Adizdo Pan African Dance Ensemble (1984-2005) the central organisation for this production, had been founded by George Dzikunu and Emmanuel Tagoe, both dance specialists from among the Ewe and Ga ethnic groups in Ghana; the executive director, Zagba Oyortey is Krobo also from the Eastern part of Ghana. This production of a 53 cast had as its artistic director, Geraldine Conor, the famous director of *Carnival Messiah* originally from Trinidad and Tobago and, British. The script was written by Margaret Busby with Ghanaian and Caribbean ancestry. The partners included, the Pan African Orchestra, a 48-piece ensemble that play traditional instruments from many parts of Africa and founded in Accra by the late Nana Danso Abiam. It included the divine drummer, Kofi Ghanaba. There was also the Caribbean Music Circuit which included many Caribbean dancers and artists. [32]

The production however, was about a story - the last Anglo-Ashanti War of 1900 that took place between a small village –Ejisu and Kumasi and beyond which was led, on the Ashanti side, by Yaa Asantewaa. The musical compositions by Abiam were sung mainly by Gas from Greater Accra in Ashanti-Twi, and the dancers were of a multi-ethnic mix. The theatre design of Ashanti and Caribbean patterns was by

Conor and her group of technicians and the costume, on full coloration, were typical of the Caribbean carnival festival. [33]

It was one of the most complex but well-reviewed musical theatres in the United Kingdom. The newspapers' theatre and arts pages, were full of praises for the two-hour stage performance. The audiences were mostly white European whether at the West Yorkshire Playhouse in Leeds, Alexandria Theatre, Manchester or Edinburgh. They had read the story from the production brochure and were very consumed with everything about it. [34]

⊲◦◎———••◦◉◦   ‖   ◦◉•• •———◎◦⊳

Creative arts as the name itself suggests, is not technical science with specific answers. Artistic adaptation from the Middle East, through to Greek civilisation into Roman, European and African, had been there all the time. It is therefore not surprising that Africans born outside of the continent and with dual citizenship adapt the literary works, visual muses, music and other forms, to suit where they are and show them to audiences who would appreciate this common humanity in all arts.

Adaptations also take place internally or locally. As consumers of art become more complex - migrate from the rural areas and towns and cross classes into the middle and upper, tastes change. They see creation beyond the ethnographic into national and sometimes international, doing comparative analysis of their own. This is visible in this collection. One of the art gifts to Kufuor was from The Corporate Forum of Nigeria (*Muscular Drummer*) which is made up of corporate executives from different ethnic groups who settled on it as an ideal because to them, its aesthetic value is high. [35] This piece was one of the most difficult to photograph because, it was so well smelted and it did not matter to the Forum, which part of Nigeria and which cultural group or ethnic belief, it came from.

Of the two Benin bronze works, one was given to Kufuor by the Esama of the Benin Kingdom, Chief Gabriel O. Igbindion and therefore not surprising. [36] The other, however, was given by the District Grand Lodge of Nigeria whose elite membership again, at least not all of them, would be from Benin but wanted to gift Kufuor something depicting power for his office as the newly elected president of Ghana.

This movement in artistic taste has a parallel creation of art. In 2020 for instance, Alice Asafu-Adjaye, an architect and founder of Mustard in Accra, collaborated with Chrissa Awuah, a textile designer for the proposed London Biennale 2020 at Somerset House. Both have dual citizenship - British and Ghanaian with Awuah born and brought up in London and also having a heritage connected to Togo and Benin. With Asafu-Adjaye's University of Nottingham and

Bartlett at the UCL training, and Awuah's Chelsea School of Fine Art training, they already make an international duo in addition to their accomplishments beyond their dual nationalities. Their response, *Amplify* to the London Biennale 2020 exhibition theme of, *Resonance* was bringing Africa art to bear. Awuah's AMMA Designs is "an Adinkra-inspired homeware and interior brand" and AFRICA BY DESIGN "a concept of love intended to showcase and celebrate the best of Africa's design talents". It partly brought them together including in travels and furniture collections.

Craftsmen and industrialists could be interested in colour designs from Vietnam or silk materials from India in South Asia for their local manufacturing purposes. As well, African travellers and cloth or fashion consumers could easily be influenced by international fashion and encourage their local designers to do similar or, the same for them.

When the printing of kente patterns became industrial in the Ivory Coast from the late 1980s, and later these patterns, whether from the village of Bonwire, or elsewhere were mass developed from China, big issues were raised. Without any patent rights to designs, and seen as global folklore, did Ghanaian manufacturers have a case of international abuse of designs? Did it affect slow loom weaving production?

● Friendship of Thabo Mbeki

2010 - Johannesburg. This work was given by the eminent philosopher-king or the renaissance President of South Africa, Thabo Mbeki. Mandela's successor, he developed a strong bond with Kufuor who served as a special guest speaker when the Thabo Mbeki Foundation was launched. Mbeki and the former Managing Director of the IMF and President of Germany, Horst Kohler also helped Kufuor to launch his in Accra and Kumasi. The two had been advocates of good governance and recognised by the G-8 as observers in their deliberations during their presidencies. Though Kufuor was not part of the Troika which was behind the New Partnership for African Development (NEPAD), his government was the first to submit itself to its Peer Review Mechanism.

It had everything to do with business and international trade between the developed and developing worlds. The US Africa Trade and Opportunity Act (AGOA) was to help stem such exports from their non-indigenous origins but, it was more than just a trade policy. Whilst Africans saw many of these movements as cultural matrimony, to the world beyond it, it was a matter of demand and supply.

Would there be a manifestation of a trade policy in Ghana or other African countries? Will changing economic landscapes and varying investment codes change affect legislations within the creative industries? With the creation of the African Continental Free Trade Zone Area, would we see growth of continental aesthetics and new markets?

◁◉――・・◉◉ ||| ◉◉・・――◉▷

All these come to cultural economy or the creative economy which in globalisation has a gross production or international revenue running into trillions of dollars. Commercial art or, one as an enterprise for national revenue generation, has speeded up even in Africa which did not start with it. It is now linked to art auction houses in Europe and the Americas and there are specialists, and special houses in African art management, with universities awarding degrees in this field.

There is a rhetorical political refrain of art for cultural growth. In the last twenty-five years, policies have been built around tourism and export of cultural products including art into Europe. By the mid-2010, there were in addition to national art galleries and museums, many private ones set up by Africans or non-resident Africanists. The challenge has however been an imbalance - excellence of individual African international artists connected to the best of the world and the cultural institutions on the continent itself - infrastructure of national galleries and museums which should collectively support individuals and the private sector but which, is usually not the case.

In 2019, Ghana for the first time participated in the 58th Venice Art Biennale. It was indeed a splash as its pavilion, Ghana Freedom had been designed by the architect, Sir David Adjaye. The theme choice of, Ghana Freedom, a musical composition by the legendary E.T. Mensah, Ghana's king of Highlife music in the 1950s was originally for Ghana's Independence celebration. The adaptation shows the country's sometimes obsessive reminders as Sub-Saharan Africa's first independent country.

As the Minister of Tourism then, Catherine Afeku announced at the opening of the pavilion, *We Have Arrived*. Curated with the advice of Okwui Enwezor who worked with Nana Oforiatta Ayim, the visual and video artists were: Felicia Abban, El Anatsui, Lynette Yiadom-Boakye, Ibrahain Mahama, Selasi Awusi Sosu and John Akomfrah respectively. Kwame Anthony Appiah provided an essay for the official catalogue in this most international and global art fair. Later, there were television appearances on CNN with curator Ayim and artist Mahama on BBC and in other media. [37]

The collective powers of these individuals and as a temporary team was not, as with many situations across countries, sufficient to make Ghana or push it suddenly into an international art market of destination. They drew as it happened, the needed attention to the pavilion but the rest of the work was to be carried out through institutional and re-tuned public policies of international drive. The idea to transfer the pavilion to Accra for local audience, did not materialise a year after. The National Gallery which would ideally have hosted this had been closed down for five years and seeing its remedial repairs since 1957 when it was first opened.

In fact, of the thirty other national monuments, forts and castles that should be pillars of attraction in Ghana, some were under regeneration or also closed-down for remedial architectural works. It is one reason why an integrated public policy on restoration and further development should be a priority before the important step of marketing of these sites. The reluctance by establishment to have a structured public-private sector collaboration for needed finance equity at the same time as it talks of it as an engine for revenue generation, is itself a problem.

The Art Biennale coincided with The Year of Return which, laudable as it was and successful to some extent, had hindrances with institutional inadequacies. Ghana with more monuments on the Trans-Atlantic Slave Trade than other West African countries, had a better attraction. The Year of Return Project under the Ministry of Tourism Culture and Creative Arts had an ancestry - The Joseph Project in 2007, the year of Ghana's Golden Jubilee as a sovereign country. Both sought to exploit African-American tourists and potential investors into the country though The Year of Return was better marketed.

With low government budget support, this problem cuts across. Creative industries are asked to be internal revenue mobilisers without infrastructure support. Again, partnership with a vibrant private sector becomes difficult as legislation, parliamentary approval and re-structuring or the never completed public sector reforms, are big issues.

⬟ Mandela and 'The Hope of Africa' Art

2010- Johannesburg. Africa hosted the historic World Cup for the first time in South Africa for what was a further healing in post-Apartheid. Having failed as host nation and with all African teams eliminated, the Black Stars of Ghana became 'The Hope of Africa' as it got to the quarter finals before it was also eliminated by Uruguay on penalties. Nelson Mandela, very impressed with the Black Stars performance invited the team to his palatial home in Johannesburg on July 3 2010 and thanked them on behalf of Africa. This special painting from the Mvezo Komkhulu cultural centre in Johannesburg serves as a memorial. A flag of Ghana, its leadership through the black star symbol and with a team captain bearing the hopes and aspirations of a continent.

Chapter Eight

Not for Its Sake

Decorative art by name implication could be homely: elements of interior designs such as living room furniture - of sofas, posh cedar or mahogany, upholsteries with gold or bronze alignment, hand-made and woven carpets and depending on the individual, wooden or metallurgic bookshelves, pottery or vases and where one has, a garden with chairs and plant tending little tools. Class and taste are associates and the more exotic ones speak volumes: Rolex furniture, Hermes silk art products and more.

The older the better. In antique shops, out of fashion art and related products have exclusive prices. Decorative galleries of small stature and ancient ones of their kind are across inner urban quarters like Soho, Bloomsbury and Mayfair in London or opposite the Elysee Palace in Paris or metropolitan Antwerp. Of course there is the dotted art city of Venice. The auction houses of Sotheby's and Christie's (including their international ones) had existed long enough for middle and upper class trading in the exotics.

Today, they are not just Eurocentric or Anglo-Saxon acquisitions but to some, of global middle class status. Many wealthy and intellectual French-speaking Africans and the Caribbean including the Senegalese President, Leopold Sedar Senghor, were not just metropolitan patrons but famous poets of Negritude respectively. The best of France including architecture and locations in the south especially Normandy and its beaches, impressed their sensibilities.

If you visit the Manhyia Palace in Kumasi, with its known conservative outlook, the decorative art is predominantly Ashanti including furniture items but you will also find either in the big living room or dining room, cabinets of cutlery that are world prized, a collection of fascinating sets of tea cups in its room as well as Persia carpets. But even before this panorama of inner palace decoration, you are likely to see a flock of peacocks about, sprouting their feathers and screeching. These are possible breeds from the original ones from the Shah of Iran before the Iranian revolution in 1979, for the late Asantehene Otumfuo Opoku Ware II.

Not All Stools Are Thrones

1999 - Kumasi. To visually inspire Kufuor to live up to his dream of the presidency, he was presented with a replica presidential or state chair by the Asantehene Otumfuo Osei Tutu II. (See first chair 1 on the right) The original was created by the artist Kofi Antubam in 1957 and has since been the ceremonial chair of presidents of four Republics for their swearing-in ceremonies and addresses to parliament. In the heat of the 1992 election in which J.J. Rawlings as military leader contested against other opposition leaders and later Kufuor, he said those who wanted to sit on the chair, that is unseat him should go to Anloga in Kumasi (his Ewe kinsmen operate a craft and furniture village and also Kufuor's home region) and make for themselves one. Its implicit meaning was, it would be difficult to give power away. To some Ghanaians this was contempt to the democratic transition.

2004- Côte d'Ivoire/Ivory Coast. In ethnography, chairs and stools have specific purposes even in their functional similarity. This chair (see second chair on the right 2) from Sakasu in the Ivory Coast or La Côte d'Ivoire and similar in design to the *Aspim* of the Ashanti (*Kiti cha enzi* in Swahili). With the same traditional chieftaincy institutions (the result of centuries old migration)

the Baoule Akan are found in Bouake and Yamoussoukro where the first President of Ivory Coast, Felix Houphouet-Boigny came from. Like the Akan of Ghana, their kindred in southern Ivory Coast made wealth as cocoa farmers. Apart from traditional governance structure, linguistics, and most visible of all, visual art of wooden sculpture, patterns and designs of Kente or Adinkra cloth are shared heritage. Some of the weavers in the Kwabre district of Ashanti even trace their ancestry to the Baoule.

Kufuor, a great admirer of Houphouet-Boigny played a major role in bringing peace to Ivory Coast before and after its civil war. This chair was given partly in appreciation.

The Sakasu carver is probably a Catholic with his choice of colours and a crucifix pinned to the upper head-rest of the chair.

Consecrated black stools of the Akan (see third stool, 3 on the right) are normally in a mausoleum of kings and queens with veneration rites every forty days - during the Akwasidae festival. The sacred stools are different from those for domestic purposes. The last smaller one also from the Ivory Coast and coloured yellow is different by coloration from a Ghana made which is either a polished wood or blackened.

1.

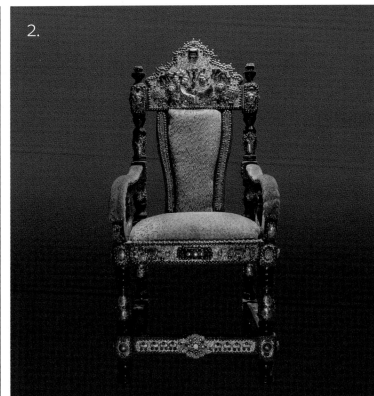

2.

3.

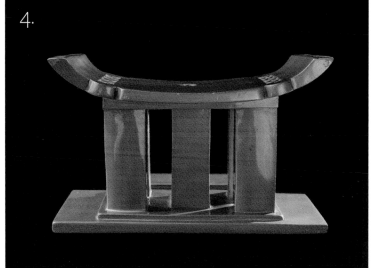

4.

The current, Osei Tutu II lived for years in infatuation among the elite grandeur of London and considers the place and his country-cottage in Oxfordshire, a second home.

Like Kufuor before him in age, the Asantehene and his friend like their friend, the former UN Secretary-General Kofi Annan, grew up in Ashanti New Town from the 1960s. The world was not that knitted. The art collection of Kofi Annan and his artist wife Nane, as expected are global and some were sold when he was alive, for philanthropic causes.

Yet, when in August 2002, Osei Tutu II decided to honour him with the title of Busumburu, the great sword of which he swore the oath of allegiance and without which he could not have become an Asantehene, it was the first and only time in over 300 years that it had been bestowed on an individual who happened to be the first black Secretary-General of the UN. Annan in the most remembered durbar for the occasion wore a cloth - Ntam partly white coloured as he mostly did on visits to the palace: a balance of tradition and global personage.

If the Busumburu title was an incentive for added vigour and further achievement, a chair given Kufuor by the same Asantehene before then was meant to serve the same purpose. Though not original, the chair was meant as a proverbial gift. A replica of the presidential chair that the state artist, Kofi Antubam created in 1957 for Kwame Nkrumah and the newly independent state, it is very Akan in concept with the use of Adinkra motifs. It is the official symbol of state or presidential power after swearing-in and when on occasions, a president addresses the nation.

In the heat of the 1992 presidential election and when JJ Rawlings, Ghana's military ruler decided to contest, he remarked to the condemnation of some Ghanaians that, his opponents should get for themselves a similar chair and not the original. To some critics, it meant that he would win the elections through fair or foul means. He did not only win but was re-elected in 1996. But the Asantehene not amused presented Kufuor with a replica. It was, like the Busumburu, to inspire his goal. He became the first civilian President of Ghana's Fourth Republic and the most successful conservative leader since 1948.

The chair is a massive decorative art of over 100 kilogrammes and sits at a corner of the entrance to Kufuor's study. To those who know, it's art but with spiritual aura from one with some interest. The French philosopher, Victor Cousin's sacramental approach of, "L' Art pour I'art", whose famous translation is 'art for art sake' in which any piece of art needs no explanation, should not be loaded with didactics or in-built histories or utilitarian goals, does not apply in most of Africa. Indeed, even in European art and history as in for example Simon

Schama's career as a distinguished British-Jewish art historian and philosopher, he and kindred in the industrial sector need these; whether to explain Bernini's cathedral architecture in Rome or the basis of Rembrandt the Dutch master's work in The Netherlands.

Back to Ghana, you will find what is also to the casual observer, another decorative art when in a state sitting and surrounded by other chiefs and sub-chiefs, a mat of zebra skin is spread before the Asantehene. You will see besides it a special wooden foot-rest decorated with animal skin and sewed to the edges. Whilst the zebra mat is exclusive to him, other chiefs have those of sheep skin. After the killing of a sheep, the entire skin is carefully removed by an expert, washed and sprinkled with wooden ashes (against insect infection) and then tied to a rectangular wood with nails to dry. A couple of days after, it is done.

The popular foot-rest sold in the markets are traditionally made from donkey skin in the northern parts of Ghana and the Sahel. Again the donkey skin is removed and sewed to bigger sizes such as these (see right hand-side, Zebra Mat). Where donkey skin is not used that of cattle is. They are then stuffed with cotton and dyed to give the desired colour effect.

⬟ Zebra Mat

2005 - Ghana. Part of the regalia of Akan governance, it was in the ancient times made from the skin of Zebra for Asantehenes. This material is today difficult to access because of the dwindling Zebra population but few Kenyan merchants trade and export it. Other animal mat versions like this one - with sheep skin are for other chiefs. The sheep skin is carefully removed, sprinkled with wood ash and tied to a rectangular wood board to dry.

● Foot-rest

2005 - From northern Ghana and made
of the skin of a donkey and stuffed with
cotton, the skin of a cow could sometimes
be used.

⬟ Elmina Castle

2016- Elmina Castle. This is a contemporary 2016 painting of the Elmina Castle by an artist in Kumasi, Nana Baafi Adomako. A protégé of the well-known public artist of the city, Alex Amofa of Supreme Art Works, this is one of the biggest of Ghana's forts and castles built by the Portuguese in 1482. It was used as a temporary shelter for slaves. It was at various times a trading depot for European merchants and as an administrative facility of colonial rule. It has a shared history of the Salaga slave market in northern Ghana through Kumasi into its coastal location. To Adomako, it is also a reminder of the British colonial officers intended place of exile for the Asantehene, Nana Agyeman Prempeh I in 1897. He and his exiled entourage were later taken to Freetown, Sierra Leone and eventually to the Seychelles Islands. It is as a tourism site one of the sources of revenue generation for the Ghana Museums and Monuments Board.

In big global art auction houses, there are usually hundreds of departments or specialised periodic portfolios. A European department alone could have periods stretching through centuries of art development. There are works as ancient as one thousand years old, whether as cathedrals or the so-called 'Museums of England' such as the Salisbury Cathedral whose 800th anniversary was recently celebrated, through to the Reformation, Victorian, Napoleonic and from impressionism of painting to modern or contemporary art. You would also find Occident and Orient departments, Islamic departments and the Americas and Africa.

Notwithstanding the departmentalisation of art, they refuse to be so departmentalised and they can also be made into decorative or memorial art. Jews who suffered the holocaust and remembered family tragedies, if they were artists, drew them and could have them as decorative art in their homes or family houses. The same events or transitions led painters to the facilities or monuments through which and at where some of these atrocities occurred: whether in Auschwitz in Poland because it was a great concentration camp, or other parts of Europe where some escaped to and had their impressions of their troubles, exile, dispossession and suffrage immortalised. These could be as personal as they could be public art in the sense that they occupy, whether as statues, graffiti or wall painting, public places and consciousness. They could in fact also be classified as holocaust art.

During the Slave Trade, from the time of capture of the slaves in small African villages in the internecine wars to the African continental coastlines, particularly in West Africa, and through the voyage across the Atlantic into the Americas, a whole movement of art school, practitioners and agitators was generated. Their evolution reflected the 400-year old history of this atrocious occurrence. If the dispersal of the Jews took place from Europe where they were technically seen as not belonging, the slave trade in Africa was the uprooting of those belonging and by brute force and collaboration from within. The Jews would split globally as the Africans would become African-Americans in the United States' new world. Others would go to the Americas and the Caribbean, the Middle East and as far as Iraq.

The over one hundred and fifty slave narratives whether of Equiano Olaudah or Harriet Tubman and glimpses given, would help define the sociology of their immediate arrival. This was through oral traditions and later personal experiences. The influences of the first Africans who landed in Virginia and in the plantation economies of the South added to this. The art of their survival (whether the cotton fields and landscape, or their cabins of abode) are as important as the monuments connected to their forebears' departure from Cape Coast and Elmina in the Gold Coast or the Gorêe Island in Senegal.

Alabama- Another Country

2005 - Harlem, New York. The author purchased this oil painting on hard board from an African-American street art dealer. An 1800s family house possibly in rural Alabama in the Southern United States, its connection to Harlem of the past is also striking. A family of six and a newly arrived baby, the mother engages in drying of fabrics and washing of others whilst a presumed husband relaxes on the porch of this two-room shotgun house. This architecture some historians believe, is a memory-carriage of early African slaves in the Americas; particularly those from the West Coast of Senegal and The Gambia.

Unless the two ladies in conversation are visiting, it's a bit of a crowded accommodation in what looks like the beginning of a fall or autumn. African-Americans like rural dwellers in most places, reared livestock and had backyard gardens to supplement their food needs. We see chicken out of their coop; there is a storage and a farm carriage.

The title of James Baldwin's novel, Another Country is so apt with this. As recently as 1997, one could enter Montgomery, the capital of Alabama at sunset from Atlanta, Georgia in near darkness, virtually no street and neighbourhood lighting system in clusters of shotgun architectures.

⬠ Of Paul Gauguin

The French stockbroker and financer who became an influential painter and artist, Paul Gauguin was underestimated when alive. Today, he is one of the most valued in terms of global art market rankings and an early European in the 1880s who saw Africa and Asia-Pacific as new frontiers. His decision to travel and live in the French Island of Martinique which is over 80% African and mixed race, produced fascinating paintings. *Tahitian Women on the Beach* (1891) the original of which is in the collection of Musee d'Orsay in Paris was during his Asia-Pacific sojourney. It's a pose and sand shore beach leisure situation of the sitters who are in formal dress at an empty (of people) beach. This photographic version is from a digital copy of the author's. It was created for sale by Frechmann Kolon GmbH.

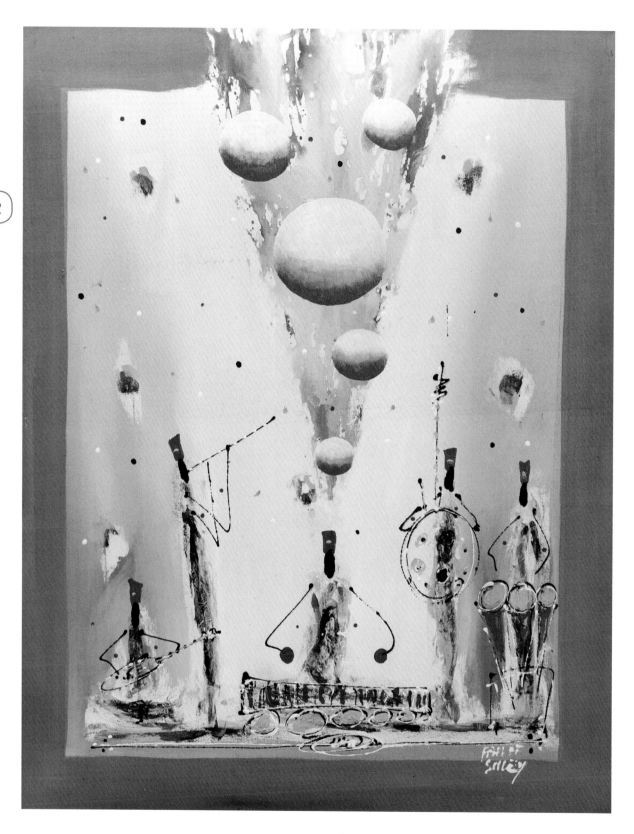

Gift of Music and The Abolitionists

2019- Accra. One of Africa's gifts to the new world of the Americas was music- the development of Negro Spirituals- the likes of, *We Shall Overcome Someday* and *Go Tell It On the Mountains* and of course the surrealism of Jazz. They were connected to the story of the Trans-Atlantic Slave Trade even if the Harlem Renaissance of the 1920s served as the golden age. This painting is a modern reminder; a musical fiesta with five musicians and a set of instruments, a trumpet, guitar, xylophone, a drum major and a set of three drums with a lighting effect typical of a Jazz festival in the Caribbean. The humanity that created a cheap international labour system for capitalist exploitation in Europe and the Americas through the slave trade was the same that led to its abolition. In all, music was comforting of the troubles at the plantation economies in the South.

⬠ Colours of Meanings

2019- Accra. This is a painting of eight-colours and multiple symbolisms across ethnographic cultures. In the eyes of colour theorists, it could be associated or form the corpus of West Africa batik or fabric art, - the popular Woodin in Ghana, Ivory Coast and Nigeria. Indigenous originally to the Asia-Pacific region of Java in Indonesia, West African soldiers had fought there in the 1940s and returned home with batik fabric that would influence its development. These same colours could remind others of Islamic art including some of the Lots auctioned at Roseberys in London in June 2020. In the Far East, they could be colour templates for traditional Japanese painting.

That period of dispersal and acculturation was also of interest to other artists during the colonial period that followed from the mid 1800s in Africa. Colonial rule them was the reverse as the artists instead went to the colonies.

The paintings of the French stockbroker and journalist, Paul Gauguin is most instructive. Not recognised in the art traditions of his time in Paris, he grew frustrated by that and what he thought was limited license for creativity in the homeland. He was one of the early Europeans (and distantly with Van Gogh) who saw Africa and Asia-Pacific as opening societies with vistas of creations. His residence as artist in the French Island of Martinique in the 1880s (which is 80% African and is multiracial) and in the Pacific Island of Tahiti are counted among his fruitful times. It did not matter that he died almost a pauper though his works are among the most expensive in the markets today.

Again back home in Ghana and Africa and in time. Between 2006 and 2007 when the world celebrated the bi-centenary of the abolition of Slave Trade, Kufuor participated in Ghana and abroad. He was invited to be guest speaker at the Wilberforce Institute of Slavery and Emancipation at the University of Hull and would deliver the Roscoe Lecture and receive an honorary fellowship from Liverpool's John Moores University in 2007. The Deputy Prime Minister of Britain, John Prescott was also in Ghana to celebrate the event and visited some of the slave monuments.

● William Wilberforce

2007. Yorkshire. Four of this pot were made of clay from the Kingston upon Hull Yorkshire home of the abolitionist, politician and art collector, William Wilberforce. One was presented to Queen Elizabeth II and another to the Archbishop of York and Primate of England, John Suntum. Suntum had himself suffered prison sentence under slavery conditions during Idi Amin's dictatorship in Uganda and later gained his freedom and went into exile in Britain. He studied at Cambridge and into the Anglican priesthood. From his diocese in York which Wilberforce served as Member of Parliament of Hull in 1785, Suntum's interest in the fundamental rights of all humanity is known. He presented this third pot to Kufuor with the fourth going to the Wilberforce Institute for the Study of Slavery and Emancipation which was established at the University of Hull in 2006. It was officially opened by Kufuor with the Nobel laureate and Archbishop of Cape Town, Desmond Tutu as its Chief Patron.

Whilst condemnation of slavery was everywhere including its modern form of child labour and trafficking, Kufuor painted a heinous verbal picture of the Trans-Atlantic Slave Trade and alerted minds in Liverpool in his lecture, *Human Rights and the Citizen.* He went back over 2,000 years to the Old Testament times of slavery and commended the society in the New Testament who rectified slavery conditions. He even cited Aristotle's *Politics* the political philosophy treatise in which the Greek said, "Humanity is divided into two - the masters and the slaves."

His commendation spread from the biblical to Roscoe whose lecture series was inaugurated with one from the Dalai Lama, Tenzin Gyatso at John Moors' and William Wilberforce for a system of evil that "helped to define human evolution in the nature of an ancient problem." Long before the dramatic occurrence of the Trans-Atlantic, there was the coming of American libertarians like its third President, Thomas Jefferson; with contradictions as slave owners whilst they sought in the same breath its abolition. In this short detour of a chapter and flexibility of instances - people, leadership and geniuses that defined the world they lived in, events and milestones of history soaked with blood and also with glory, the motives of capitalism and neo-capitalism, faith and ideology, could all become monuments of interest through public art. They needed to be explained in original thinking and in contemporary sense and beyond, and not the periphery dictum of art for its sake.

Chapter Nine

Cloth of Many Colours

Ali Mazrui in "Tools of Exploitation", the fourth part of his *The Africans - A Triple Heritage* television series, visually made clearer the damage that the Trans-Atlantic Slave trade did to Africa's indigenous cottage industries. The 'evil triangle' of the slaves who provided enormous labour on the cotton plantations in the Americas (including in the economies of the Carolinas), saw the harvest shipped to Industrial Revolution Britain and western Europe. Here, textile manufacturing would take place and some of the products would later be exported to Africa for consumption.

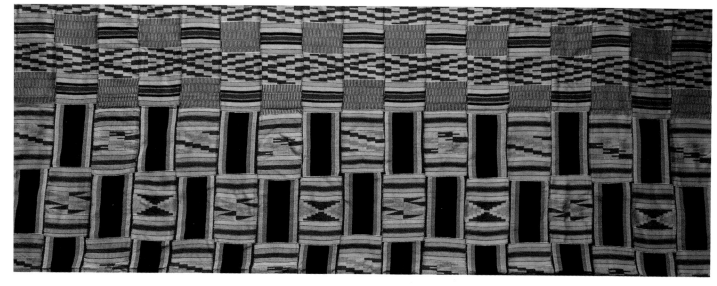

Kente

2010 – Kyeretwie or **Oyokoman**, Bonwire, Ashanti. The choice of a design or colours for weaving of a kente cloth has carefully and purposefully been done in over three centuries of industrial practice. Almost all cloths have names connected to important individuals: community leaders, religious figures, responsible family and clan heads, presidents, kings and queens, or events of defining times.

This is the famous "Kyeretwie" or Oyokoman design created decades ago and has mutated in fashion. The presenters from Bonwire had a higher sense of Kufuor's lineage. Kyeretwie or more appropriately, Osei Kyeretwie is the name of the Asante King, Otumfuo, Sir Osei Agyeman Prempeh II, who re-cre-

ated the Ashanti confederacy in 1935. Respected when alive and in history, Asantes including Kufuor paid their allegiance to him. But the king became Kufuor's brother-in-law when he got married to his sister, Agnes Addo Kufuor. Of their two children, Oheneba Kwame Kyeretwie, whom the king named after himself, that is Kufuor's nephew, became the chief of Apagya or Apagyafie in Kumasi.

The cloth's other name, Oyokoman identified the king with the ruling clan of Ashanti or the Akan. Kufuor's father, Nana Kwadwo Agyekum who was the Oyokohene or chief of the clan is thus associated with the cloth as well. Kufuor wore this cloth on important occasions.

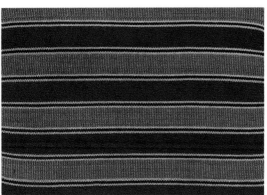

1976 - Bonwire, Ashanti. This cloth (top of page) is also called "Kyeretwie" or "Oyokoman" but it is woven in different colours. It is a typical 1970s make of pure cotton. As with all kente cloths, this has different strips joined to make a 12-yards piece for a man's wear. It has nine strips. The dominant wine-red coloured strips alone has one hundred and eighty strip pieces and the eight others are of the same number, making a total of about one thousand four hundred and twenty pieces. In designing other variations, some of the strips are mutated in reverse. They are then given a name.

The similarity between this and the one on the left is that, they were purposely made. This one was made for a royal of Asante Mampong, Joseph Agyeman-Duah, who happened to be the secretary of Otumfuo, Sir Osei Agyeman Prempeh II and his successor, Opoku Ware II. Agyeman-Duah's father was from the royal house of Bonwire and this was made for his wedding. These presidential clothes (of the early 2000s) and this 46-year old one were status productions: compact at the end edges unlike the current loosened detached ones.

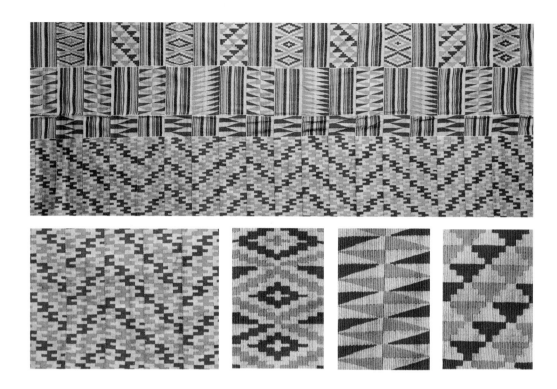

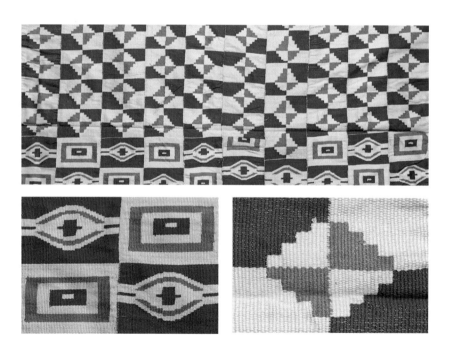

2010 – Bonwire, Ashanti. This and the one immediately below are called *Adwene si adwene so* and translated as multiple motifs or designs. In the language of the craftsmen, it is popular as design upon design. It's a show of the ability of designers to turn colours and thoughts around. Presented by weavers fascinated with the social policy interventions that Kufuor made during his presidency.

Of course, colonial rule created overseas African markets for industrial products besides exploitation of raw materials and labour. The African markets meant, where possible, application of brute force as in the Belgium Congo for consumption of these exports. The secondary effect was the alteration of choices against the inherent infrastructure of indigenous textile production and clothing.

In West Africa, industries existed before the Industrial Revolution of the 1860s. Ashanti, before it became part of the Gold Coast colony from 1900, had its famous industrial village of Bonwire producing since the 1700s what is now a global fashion commodity - Kente. There had been evidence, for centuries, of shared industrial creative thoughts and designs in clothing between Ashantis and the people of the Ivory Coast especially in its northern part.

There were other villages in the Trans-Volta or now Agotime-Kpetoe in the Volta region engaged in similar production based on centuries old histories and cultures in nearby countries of Togo and Benin.

When Mazrui argues that parts of African civilisation including its manufacturing bases were not well-known before contact with Europeans, it poses the question as to whether it was ever a motivation. These inventions of palace art and the manufacturing sectors were basically for indigenous needs. They captured histories for the benefits of incoming clans, and of an economy that was basic to livelihoods. Yes, there was international trade among Africans and internal exploitation of labour in post-ethnic war situations which explains the participation of Africans in the slave trade; but, the motivation had also been the growth of the lineage.

In the performing arts of the Gold Coast, two ethnomusicologists and artists from the 1930s whose sociology of music most exemplified heritage and heritage economics (incidentally without as much a plan to get to the world of ethnomusicology but did get there at the end) were, Ephraim Amu and his mentee, J.H. Kwabena Nketia. Amu's industrial music - Bonwire Kentenwene - an Ode to the Kente Cloth or Asante Bonwire Kente, was about the manufacturing process of the kente cloth during a visit he made to Bonwire, near Kumasi as a student in the 1920s.

Nketia was a Presbyterian and an alumnus of the Basel Mission School or Presbyterian Teacher Training College, which had been established in Akropong, in the Eastern region of Ghana in the 1830s. As Christians, they sought to incorporate, against colonial resistance to African cultural values of music composition, indigenous musical instruments and kente as a dress code in church worship. These were not encouraged by the European missionaries but these revolutionaries were strengthened by other progressives such as the Catholic Bishop of Kumasi, Peter Kwasi Sarpong. This very difficult transition

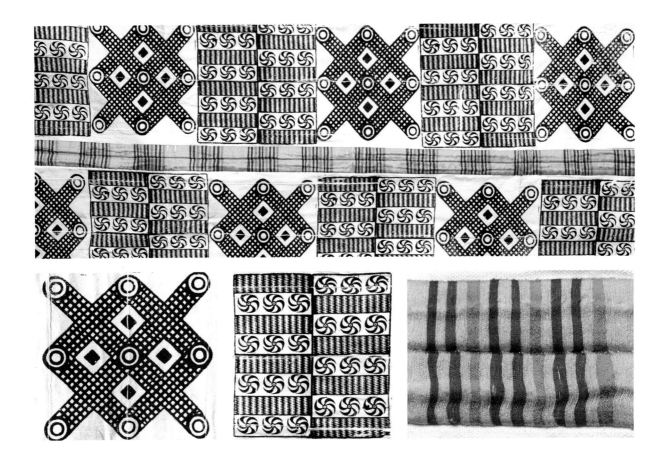

⬟ Calligraphy of a Cloth

2005 – Kwabre, Ashanti. This piece is called *Adinkra ɛna Ɔkodeɛ Bɔwerɛ* — an Adinkra cloth with the finger nails of an eagle. The history of Adinkra symbols in Ghana is an earlier manifestation of artistic writing and development of vocabulary. These symbols were adopted in the manufacturing of what is called Adinkra cloth but sometimes related in design to Kuntukuna in Ashanti. The manufacturing also existed in the Ivory Coast centuries ago through associated Ashanti imperial wars. Together with goldweights, they are proverbial as well. In the Kwabre district and parts of the Central region of Ghana, Adinkra or Kuntukuna cloth is a big rural industry.

As black and white colours have come to signify happiness, achievement, immortal goodness, Kufuor wore this on a number of occasions.

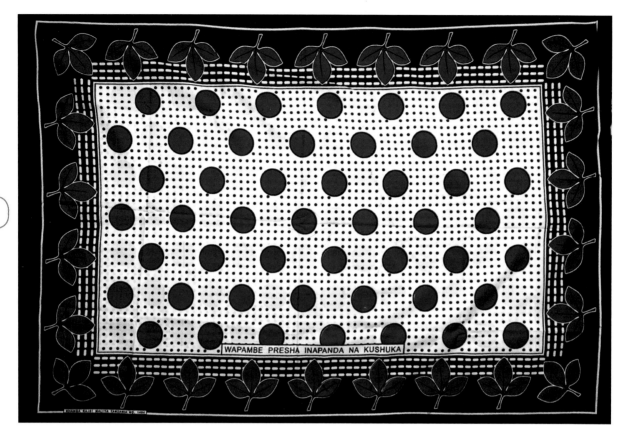

⬟ Misfortune

2014 – Tanzania, East Africa. The Somali-based Islamic fundamentalist group, al-Shabaab invaded the Westgate Mall in Nairobi, killing 71 people including the Ghanaian poet, Kofi Awoonor. The following year undaunted by the incident, The Storymoja organisers invited Awoonor's contemporary, the Nobel laureate Wole Soyinka to give The Wangari Maathai Memorial Lectures, under very tight security in a packed hall in memory of Awoonor, who could not fulfil the previous invitation. After the event, Soyinka was presented with this Tanzanian cloth with the Swahili inscription - *Wapambe Presha Inapanda Na Kushuka,* roughly translated as, protagonists of hatred prepare the grounds for their heart illness and demise. As tragedy or misfortune is part of life, Africans sometimes symbolise events of good and evil import in designs. This cloth was re-gifted to the author by Soyinka.

which helped Christianity to take roots for what could have eventually led to its collapse, is now taken for granted.

It is ironic that post-independent Ghana and Africa had prototypes of the textile factories in Britain and The Netherlands as part of the state enterprises in the 1950s and '60s. It was at a time when state driven industrialisation or import substitution as a driver of growth was a popular model of development in especially the South. They produced print wax- Akosomobo Textiles, Dumas and others, at the industrial town of Tema in Ghana. As pride was taken in the display of indigenous clothing like kente and smock from northern Ghana, the cottage industrial bases were not expanded or set on industrial patterns. Still, they survived and by the time of the second structural change of the Ghanaian economy in 1983, privatisation of state enterprises would be and many of these industries would collapse or have to be absorbed into the private sector.

Bonwire in the Ejisu-Juaben Municipality, with its current population of over 10,000 survives other cottage industrial villages and towns of over three centuries. They do because they were mainly set-up as private sector manufacturing hubs. In the Kwabre, Kwabre East and West districts with major towns such as Mamponteng, Asonomaso and Ntonso, also known for the Adinkra crafts, these towns make a population of over 350,000. They had endured and developed with these industries as main sources of income and through that, diversified the districts' economies – with rural banks and suppliers' credits, schools and colleges, agriculture and retail shops as well as transportation systems to major towns and cities across the country, and to telecommunication networks.

In terms of employment (and apart from agriculture), this cottage industry - loom builders, weavers, suppliers (locally and from Asia of raw materials, due to the closure of cotton factories in northern Ghana) and the sellers, make the industry of the Kente, Kuntukuna and Adinkra cloths. It is pure cultural economy you see beneath the cloth of many colours woven on ancient looms; they are not just beautiful but proverbial and of historical recollections of the receded past and present. Artists keep developing new patterns different from those of the 1950s, 1970s and 1990s. There are even inverse designs of the Adinkra marks and revisitations of the old design patterns of the 1950s.

When Kufuor became president, he received some of these cloths of many colours from the palace of the King of Asante, from the Chief of Bonwire and other individuals of good standing in society, perhaps more than he could store. Some were even dedicated by way of design to his presidency and certain defining social measures he took. These were not new adorations, for in the Kumasi of his youth and opposite or within the Apagyafie neighbourhood, there are still stores that are trading in cloth.

It's very common to see people going to Manhyia from the area then and now on Mondays and Thursdays in their black clothes. Hearing of civil cases, chiefship disputes, swearing-in of new chiefs and destoolments are part of the palace calendar. Both sides of his family - of a mother (queenmother) and father (the chief of the Oyoko clan) had regular supplies of these cloths of many colours and so he was naturally brought up to understand the cultural nuances.

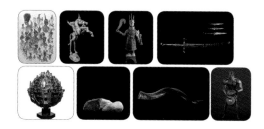

Chapter Ten

Eyes of the Beholder

All have eyes and sensors with which to see and feel. But things and particularly works of art are not seen the same way. Often what is appreciable, or to use the word beautiful, depends on many factors: first, the environment in which people live. What is beautiful could only be what they know within and can see. In the art of popular cargo or commercial transport in Africa, there is, *Travel and See*. The connotation is, if you are encased in your small village and have not travelled, you only know what is around you. In that situation, your sensors lack comparative reflex.

In many agrarian societies, farmers talk of the greenness of the veg-etation and how delighted they are to see rainfall blossom their sprouting crops. They can't wait for a coming harvest. When they give farm product gifts and smoked edible meat to city dwellers, they do so with the best of the harvest. They feel blessed to give out even if not for money; it would still not be for perish.

Within this same environment, the beauty or otherwise of the symbolism of faith is determined by adherents and non-adherents. When a Catholic or Anglican admires to the high heavens, a painting of the *Adoration of the Shepherds* or *The Virgin Mary,* it may mean nothing to another Christian of the Pentecostal or Charismatic sect. To Christian orthodoxy including of the Eastern, Jewish transferred rituals into Christianity, the role of Mary the mother of Jesus, the rit-uals of Lent and their symbolism are central matters. To that extent, Jane Williams's in *The Art of Lent,* is not like any other omnibus art book. The theologian of King's College London and wife of the for-mer Archbishop of Canterbury, Rowan Williams, she uses the paint-ings by respected artists to explain to a sect of Christian enthusiasts what may be of little value to others.

To a Muslim or Hindu, these highly praised artworks, may mean nothing; in religions in which symbols or paintings are seen as pa-ganism. Among Christians who value these artworks and rituals, not all collections have the same artistic merit. Some don't move them

⬟ Fanti Fashion

1874 - Cape Coast, Ghana. No foliage of female hair styles or plaits is more reflective than this: of Fanti women in the Cape Coast colony in the middle of the 1870s. Fifty women- in different sizes and shapes, with traditional headgears of those coming of age (puberty rites) are very representative of ethnographic styles among groups in what is now the Central region of Ghana. These styles have re-emerged in Ghanaian and world fashion. Some were also carried into the Americas- among African-Americans and the Caribbean.

Lady Horse-Rider

2010 - Cameroon. The difference between this woman horse-rider from Cameroon and others from the Sahel has to do with her dress code and a top hat national identification. The artist however is not only interested in her projection but her ability to control a horse in high-flight whose opened mouth and expressions show some level of agitation. This bronze art was given to Kufuor on a visit to Cameroon by President Paul Biya. In power since 1982, he is the longest serving leader in the world. It could therefore serve a proverbial purpose in governance and power play.

Art Reveals Power

December 8 2014 – Benin, Nigeria.
Benin's bronze portrait of a king
presented to Kufuor by the Esama
of Benin, Chief Gabriel O. Igbinedion
on Kufuor's 76th birthday.

as others do. *The Pieter* (in Italian) or Pity by Michelangelo has its critics: it is not representative of the Virgin Mary and her Son Jesus, they say.

Yet, in the era of globalisation, economies benefit from religious art; they and individual beneficiaries such as non-Christians in China, East Jerusalem, Vietnam and elsewhere. A lot of Christian art relics or elements—crucifix, communion chalice for the Holy Eucharist, candles, holy oil, altar design, Christmas toys whether sold in Rome, Jerusalem or other epic centres of faith, are today mostly manufactured in China. It may have one of the lowest Christian populations in the world and a history of banning churches during the peak of Mao's rule but economies of scale and labour are on its side.

If you are a pilgrim doing the Way of Sorrows in East Jerusalem, you will find that some of the people selling the rosary or the paintings of the personages of Christianity are Muslims. It is not faith they are selling but business they are engaged in and so art could be beautiful to them too. They persuade buyers with the beauty of their items. Yet, many of them do not believe in the beauty of that faith.

If it is certified and it is difficult to know who and exactly how it got coined, the phrase, "Beauty Lies in the Eyes of the Beholder", in whatever mutation it has travelled, (from Greece most likely and perhaps under one of the Platonic philosophies from the C3rd), its popularisation in Europe and the Americas is but an apt feeling. Most of humanity assume this in different ways and manners. People did not need to know Greek, Roman or European philosophies. In many proverbs among societies in Africa, this human condition is adequately explained:

Anomaa ho bɛyɛ fɛ a, na efiri ne ntakara

If a bird is beautiful, it is so because of its feathers.

(Fine feathers make a fine bird) [38]

There is another proverb also from the Ashanti:

Awirikwaa se adee a eye fe ye fe, nti na ode ne kokoo abo nemoma so

The green parrot says that something which is beautiful is beautiful, that is why it puts its red on its forehead.

(Everybody uses beauty to adorn themselves if they can). [39]

I have cited these proverbs in their Twi dialect or language (before their translation) as ancient expressions and part of the immemorial language development of the people and the beauty they conceived around them.

Malian Sword

December 2006 - Mali's military weaponry dates
back to the reign of Sundiata, the King of Savannah or The Lion of Mali who before he died in
1225 was a strategist in governance in the Sahel.
These three different knives or swords (as examples) in their sheath possibly originated from his
time. It was given on a State visit to Mali in addition to a white horse that was brought to Ghana
as a gesture of the visit. Unfortunately, the horse
got afflicted with a disease and died.

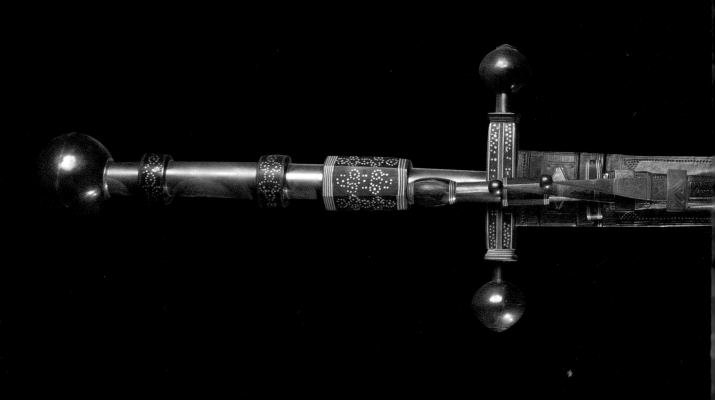

⬠ Remember Jerusalem

January 2001- East Jerusalem. One of the early art works Kufuor received in the month of his inauguration as the first civilian President of Ghana's Fourth Republic was this and from his Jew friend, Isaac Yardeni of the West Africa Projects Limited. It is an aerial view by the sculptor of East Jerusalem and its concentration of major monuments and symbols of the Abrahamic religions. Made of bronze, it is very representative of the origins of faith and conflicts. If you are travelling into East Jerusalem from Galilee, you pass through Jericho and you arrive literally through a gate, as this art work with its door into the epic of the monuments shows.

Stone Art

2013 - Galilee. This is stone art of a sort - natural little monuments with a constitution of shape and faith aesthetics. It
was collected by the author from the Sea of Galilee which is
between the Golan Heights and Galilee. Apart from stones
washed ashore by the sea, much of human habitation and
historical episodes in parts of The Middle East are in the
reckoning against nature: the drying up of River Jordan
and the dislocation of The Road to Ephesus and its famous
passage of the angels are examples. With its seashore now
popular with secular tourists and consumers of daily harvest of tilapia fish, the faithful pick its stones and wash their
faces with pristine water. Will it be art and calligraphy that
will help in memory restoration or human changes that
may prevail?

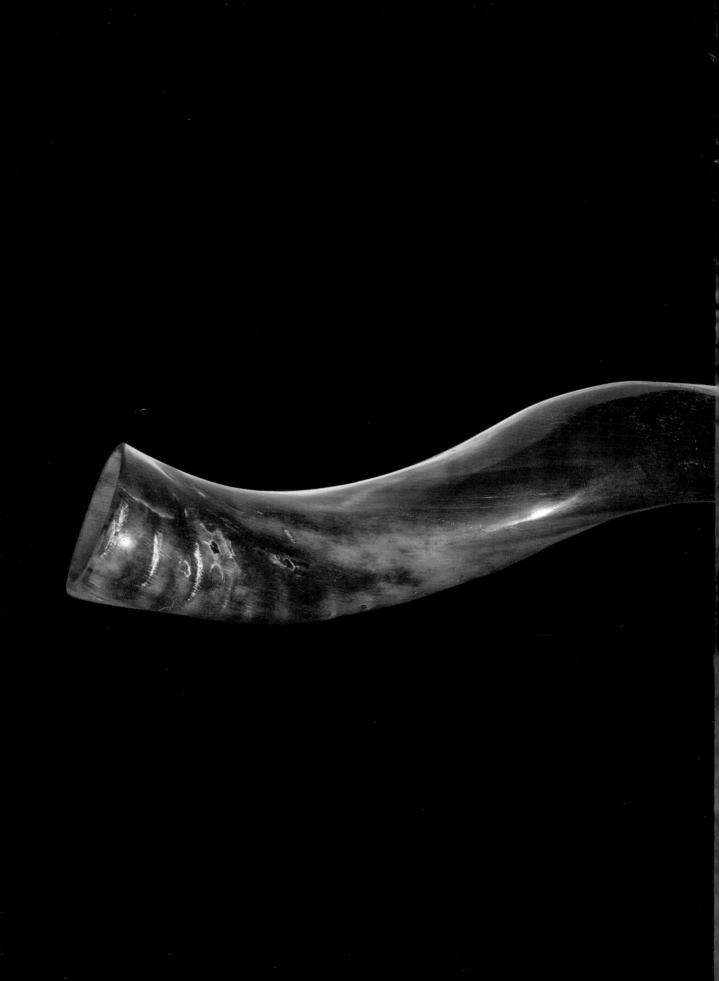

Horn from Judea

2010 - Galilee, Israel. There are many biblical allusions especially in The Old Testament of the role that animals: sheep, cattle and others play in Jewish faith and history aside being for human consumption. As not all animal parts are edible, some like a horn of a sheep or cattle or trunk of an elephant becomes a cultural item for individuals and institutional decoration. They could be ceremonial horns and part of a set of musical or collective ensemble as one that might have been played for Kufuor's father-the Oyokohene on occasions. This one under reference was given to him by a Jew. It is sometimes difficult, without being told, which horn came from which society as all animals with them have about the same features.

Muscular Drummer

January 7 2017. Nigeria. Drums have their drummers. It could be difficult to differentiate between their geographic and ethnic identities. "Most drums" Zagba Oyortey, the cultural historian says, "have a wooden frame or structure, affording the drum-maker the possibility of carving symbols or figures that are distinctive and eye-catching and also signify the rank, status or lineage of the drummer." [44] Some are palace drums, sacred and occasionally for evocation of spirits and remembrances by master drummers. At outdoorings of children, during puberty rites for girls, and at funerals, drums were and are played. These would become part of African Pentecostalism. Even in times of war, it had a role as they were not originally created as art works.

This muscular professional drummer is from southern Nigeria. It was presented by the Corporate Forum of Nigeria. The complexity of its creation is intriguing, making a photographic shot of it a labour of love.

In *Fashion* in this collection, there is female fashion at the Cape Coast Castle which was part of *The Illustrated London News* in its commissioned art: 'The Ashantee War-Sketches By Our Special Artist' in 1874. [40] In this, you see Fante women of the coastal region of what is today Central region of Ghana. There are over fifty of them in different shapes and sizes, clothing of varying ethnic details particularly with hair plaits and styles and with lots of social meaning. This foliage of 1874 personifies high fashion. Cape Coast men and others would indeed see them as beautiful in their clothing. They did not know of other women elsewhere to compare and so this is the beauty they know. Over generations this would be the standard definition.

Decades after Independence, some educated elite with acquired new tastes, saw these as primitive and pre-modern. But from the 2000s onwards, and the beginning of the C21st, fashion designers, especially the youth have gone back to them. They might have been called 'tribal' or 'primitive' in Eurocentric fashion but they have a newness. It means that, the eyes of the beholder and beauty as a concept is also racially and generationally defined.

When European explorers visited Mali, they stayed with ethnic groups in Gao, Timbuktu and elsewhere. Others, particularly the British, also visited East Africa and Kenyan Maasai villages. They wrote extensively of the society and along the line, created a settler colony on the best of lands. They found men and women who wore nose, ear, mouth and stomach rings. Among the Malians and Maasai, the rings were not only rounded into their pierced body holes but were also tribal identification marks. Among the Yoruba and in the Benin Kingdom, there were the facial stratifications identifying clans as they had been among the Frafras in the northern parts of Ghana.

Though facial stratification is dying out and not compulsory in many African cultures as it used to be and in some cases outlawed, a large number of European youth and middle-aged people, wear rings in multiple holes around their faces, eyes, hairs and stomachs. Tattoos for personal, faith, gang culture and other social and religious identifications run from Portugal in Southern through Western and Central Europe and into the Americas.

Generations, in as much as they define what they want, can also pass judgement on the creations of the deceptive but mutable past. What will future generations think of the current? We may not be sure but certainly it will be along the lines of beauty in the eyes of the beholder!

Notes

1. See Kwame Anthony Appiah's, *Cosmopolitanism - Ethics in a World of Strangers* (2006), London: WW. Norton &Company.

2. Martha J. Ehrlich, *A Catalogue of Ashanti Art Taken from Kumasi in the Anglo-Ashanti War of 1874* (1981), Indiana: University of Indiana.

3. Proverbs in Africa are more than wise sayings and this particular one is also a title adaptation- *Know the Beginning Well* by KY Amoako for an economic history of Africa published by the Africa World Press, Trenton, New Jersey in 2020.

4. Anthony Appiah's, *In My Father's House- Africa in the Philosophy of Culture* (1992), London: Methuen.

5. Ivor Agyeman-Duah, *Shepherds of the New Dawn- African Literature and its Elders* (2021), North Carolina: North Carolina Academic Press.

6. See *Modern and Contemporary African Art Return to Sotheby's London* in March 2020 press release also shared by UNESCO.

7. Ibid.

8. Ivor Agyeman-Duah, 'Kufuor and Reconciliation of History' in *Daily Graphic, My Joy Online*, Accra, Ghana and *The News* in Lagos, Nigeria (December 2018) to mark his 80th birthday.

9. See the 11th R.P. Baffour Memorial Lectures delivered at the Kwame Nkrumah University of Science and Technology by Malcolm Donald McLeod under the title - *Images of Ghana: Museums, The Ownership of Cultural Property and Restitution* in Kumasi on November 25, 27 and 28, 2019.

10. Sotheby's London biography of Ben Enwonwu www.sothebys.com

11. Ben Enwonwu Foundation www.benenwonwufoundation.org

12. An excerpt from a forthcoming memoir of President Kufuor - *An African President*.

13. The English poet and hymnist, William Cowper's *Hark My Soul, it is the Lord*.

14. This poem written by the author was after a visit to the Vatican City as part of the Oxford Alumni 2018 meeting.

15. Peter Kwasi Sarpong, *Aspects of Ghanaian Ethos* (2019), Accra: Digi Books.

16. Ibid., p58.

17. Conversation with John Agyekum Kufuor, April 21, 2020, Accra Airport West.

18. Toyin Falola and Daniel Jean-Jacques, *Africa - An Encyclopedia of Culture and Society* (2016), California: ABC-CLIO.

19. Ibid.

20. Ivor Agyeman-Duah, *Yaa Asantewaa- The Heroism of An African Queen* (1999, 2007), Accra: Centre for Intellectual Renewal. Also see the television documentary of the same title.

21. John Agyekum Kufuor, "Leadership, Government and Entrepreneurship in Africa" in *Pilgrims of the Night- Development Challenges and Opportunities in Africa* (2010), Ivor Agyeman-Duah (edited), Oxfordshire: Ayebia Clarke Publishing.

22. Joseph Miezan Bognini, 'Earth and Sky' in *The Penguin Book of Modern African Poetry*, London: Penguin Books (1963) edited by Gerald Moore and Ullier Beier.

23. Mourid Barghouti, *I Was Born There, I Was Born Here* (2012), London: Walker Books.

24. Barghouti's obituary essay of Mahmoud Darwish, "He is the Son of All of You" was published in *The Guardian*, UK on August 16, 2008.

25. Amos Oz, *How to Cure a Fanatic* (2006), London: Barnes and Noble.

26. *Pavement Market* is based on a painting I bought from my regular art vendor in 2019.

27. A History of Benin Bronze.

28. Martha Judith Ehrlich's *A Catalogue of Ashanti Art Taken from Kumasi in the Anglo-Ashanti War of 1874*.

29. See British Empire Exhibition- Westminster, London: Hansard 23 April 1923.

30. Ibid.

31. Ibid.

32. Wole Soyinka, *Power, Hydropus and Other Toxic Mutations* (2013) in the Intervention Series, Ibadan: Bookcraft.

33. The official brochure of *Yaa Asantewaa Warrior Queen,* London, 1998.

34. Ibid.

35. See art work or *Muscular Drummer.*

36. See Number 39.

37. www. Universes.art/en/Venice-biennale/2019.

38. Peggy Appiah, Kwame Anthony Appiah, Ivor Agyeman-Duah, *Bu Me Be: Proverbs of the Akans* (2002, 2007), Accra and Oxfordshire: Centre for Intellectual Renewal and Ayebia Clarke Publishing.

39. Ibid.

40. The collection- *The Illustrated London News Art Work- The Ashantee War Sketches by Our Special Artist* was commissioned in 1874 by the newspaper. A set was subsequently acquired by the author through Margaret Busby and her brother in the 2000s.

41. See *Be Me Be.*

42. Ibid.

43. Ibid.

44. Zagba Oyortey who worked with the British Museum in London for years later became the Executive Director of the Ghana Museums and Monuments Board. He commissioned as Executive Director of Adzido in 2001 the book, *The Art of the Drum,* London which was written by Augustus Casely-Hayford.

Index